# Alcohol and You
# How to Control and Stop Drinking
# By Lewis David

©WinsPress.com 2017

Text Copyright © Lewis David 2017

All rights reserved. No part of this publication may be reproduced, or transmitted in any form or by any means, electronic or otherwise, without written permission from the author.

Cover photo © Fotolia

Legal & Disclaimer

The information contained in this book is not designed to replace or take the place of any form of medicine or professional medical advice. The information contained in this book has been compiled from sources deemed reliable, and it is accurate to the best of the Author's knowledge; however, the Author cannot guarantee its accuracy and validity and cannot be held liable for any errors or omissions. Changes are periodically made to this book. You must consult your doctor or get professional medical advice before using any of the suggested remedies, techniques, or information in this book. Upon using the information contained in this book, you agree to hold harmless the Author from and against any damages, costs, and expenses, including any legal fees potentially resulting from the application of any of the information provided by this guide. This disclaimer applies to any damages or injury caused by the use and application, whether directly or indirectly, of any advice or information presented, whether for breach of contract, tort, negligence, personal injury, criminal intent, or under any other cause of action. You agree to accept all risks of using the information presented inside this book. You need to consult a professional medical practitioner before embarking on any program or information in this book.

## About the Author

I am an addiction therapist, working in treatment centres and hospitals.

Thousands of drinkers and other drug users have attended my therapeutic groups, workshops, retreats and seminars. I have also trained treatment practitioners, police and paramedics regarding alcohol abuse.

I have written this book to share my knowledge with all the drinkers I can't see in person.

**By the Same Author**

The 10-Day Alcohol Detox Plan.

Mindfulness for Alcohol Recovery.

The Emotional Mind.

Change Your Life Today.

**Read free samples and order these books at WinsPress.com or any Amazon store.**

# Table of Contents

Introduction: Alcohol and You ................................................................ 7

1. Making a Decision ................................................................ 13

2. Seeing Through The Alcohol Scam ................................................................ 22

3. Understanding Alcohol Use Disorder ................................................................ 32

4. Exploding the Myths of Drinking ................................................................ 38

5. Choosing your Path: Moderation or Sobriety ................................................................ 49

6. Choosing Your Method: Reduction or Detox ................................................................ 58

7. Drugs That Can Help: Naltrexone and Nalmefene ................................................................ 65

8. Understanding Your Withdrawal Cycle ................................................................ 72

9. Using the Power of Time ................................................................ 78

10. Your Timeline for Change ................................................................ 87

11. Building Motivation ................................................................ 95

12. Crushing Those Cravings ................................................................ 110

13. Winning the Head Game ................................................................ 116

14. Solution Focused Thinking ................................................................ 129

15. Stopping those Spinning Wheels ................................................................ 143

16. Recruiting your Cheerleaders ................................................................ 150

17. AA and the 12-Steps ............................................................. 159

18. Smart Recovery and the 4-Point Program ........................ 168

19. Cognitive Behavioural Therapy (CBT) ............................. 176

20. Relapse Prevention ............................................................. 184

21. Now The Nightmare is Over, What Do You Want The Dream To Be? ................................................................................. 192

My Three Laws of Recovery from Alcohol Addiction. ........... 195

Bonus Chapters ......................................................................... 196

Reversing Alcoholism .............................................................. 197

Real Recovery from Alcohol Addiction ................................. 208

The Research ............................................................................. 217

But Isn't It A Disease? .............................................................. 222

Drinking and Addiction .......................................................... 230

Important New Book from Lewis David: "The 10-Day Alcohol Detox Plan" ............................................................................. 234

Finally… .................................................................................... 237

# Introduction: Alcohol and You

You know you need to do something about your drinking, but where do you start? Indeed, you might be asking yourself, can you change something that has become so central to your life, something that maybe, deep down, you love? You might be confused about whether to cut down or stop drinking, and the thought of stopping forever is terrifying.

Your motivation might be a health warning from your doctor. Maybe you are getting into trouble at work because hangovers are making you call in sick too often. Perhaps alcohol is threatening your relationships; you are having arguments with loved ones and, although you are defending your drinking, you secretly suspect that they are right. Maybe you have legal problems, a driving ban or worse. Perhaps your finances are in ruins because you spend so much money on alcohol. Or maybe you have simply reached a point where the problems alcohol brings to your life have exhausted you and you want to call time – you have had enough.

Don't worry. Whatever has brought you to this point, and whatever kind of drinker you are, you have found the right book.

I am an Addictions Therapist working every day with people who, like you, have alcohol issues. I work in one-to-one consultations with drinkers, run workshops, retreats and seminars about drinking and addiction.

More and more, I see my clients achieving great results using insights that you can't pick up from existing books on the market. This is why I wrote this book – to share my knowledge and the experiences of my clients with you in the following chapters.

This book is packed with winning ideas that my clients have tried and tested. Everything you will hear is based on solid therapeutic science. There is no ideology or dogma here, just loads of practical advice that you can put to work right away.

It doesn't matter whether you are here to reduce your drinking, to stop, or don't know which way to go. This book will help to clarify which option is best for you.

Various programs exist for people who want to deal with their alcohol difficulties. You might have heard about "12 Step" or "Cognitive Behavioural Therapy". You might have read books by former problem drinkers who have found a way to stop that has worked for them and now want you to follow their ideas. All of these different philosophies are well-intentioned and have varying amounts of success for different drinkers, but they are often contradictory and confusing for the person who just wants to stop their problem, who simply wants results.

But this book is different. It treats you as the unique human being that you are. It does not judge you or preach at you. Instead, it calmly explains the options that are open to you, so you can decide for yourself the way forward that feels right for you, the way that will produce the results you want.

Drinkers in crisis feel out of control. They don't understand why they are being compelled to drink so much and behave in ways that hurt themselves. They don't understand why they can start the day feeling awful, swearing, in total sincerity, never to drink again, only to find themselves a few hours later drunk once more. They don't understand why having a drink, instead of getting rid of the craving, just sets up a new craving to want another drink right away. They don't understand why, even though they can see the damage drinking is doing, they can't stop themselves. Alcohol seems like some huge, overpowering dark force that always gets the upper hand with them.

But it doesn't have to be that way.

To this end, we will be demystifying the whole business of drinking. I have found from spending thousands of hours working with drinkers that this works. If you understand what is going on, it cuts alcohol down to size. You start to see it for what it is, simply an addiction, and an addiction is just a habit gone wrong.

It's nothing unusual, and it's certainly nothing to be ashamed of.

People are constantly conquering addictions. Tens of millions of people have broken their addiction to nicotine, which is every bit as addictive as alcohol, probably more so. Similarly, people are constantly giving up notoriously addictive substances like heroin and cocaine, while all around you, people are moderating or stopping their alcohol use all the time.

Your drinking probably started as a small habit and in those days it may have been helpful. A little alcohol can help people overcome social anxiety, probably the most common reason why people start drinking. It can help them when life gets difficult and they need to switch off. But that little alcohol can become a lot. Then the habit turns ugly and becomes more of a problem than the problems it originally overcame. It has morphed into a powerful addiction.

Demystifying alcohol changes that. My clients find that when they understand what happens when they drink, alcohol suddenly becomes robbed of its power. Knowledge puts the power in your relationship with alcohol back in your hands. The knowledge you will get from reading to this book will give you control.

There are 21 chapters following this, and each one offers a fresh new perspective on alcohol problems. I will present the best ideas and leave you to decide which ones you want to pick up and use. I have no single philosophy to push because I don't believe any single method works for everyone. Look upon these 21 chapters as being a menu. You don't have to order every dish. Select the ones that appeal most to you, as they are the ones that are most likely to work for you.

The rewards are huge. You will become more confident and less anxious. You will learn much about yourself and discover techniques that will help you in all aspects of your life. You will become richer. You will find it easier to control your weight. You will be able to wake up with a clear head and a clear conscience, not worried about what you might have done the night before. You will be able to tell your doctor the truth when he asks you those awkward questions about your drinking. Your career will benefit. Your relationships will be better. Your mental faculties will be sharper. Your overall happiness will improve. And you might add an extra 10 or more years to your life to enjoy all these benefits.

With so much to look forward to, therefore, I would like to invite you to start thinking about controlling your drinking as something to get excited about rather than something to fear. See it as an adventure, not a chore, as a glittering prize within your grasp.

**Free PDF Download: How to Self-Diagnose Alcohol Dependency in Minutes.**

Before getting into the main body of this book, I recommend you answer a questionnaire that will show you where you are on the scale of alcohol dependency.

The questionnaire is a PDF document that I send out by email. To get a copy, all you have to do is go to webpage:

www.subscribepage.com/drinktest

and leave me the email address you want the PDF document sent to. You should receive the PDF in seconds. This is totally confidential. I don't need your name, and your email address will not be passed on to anyone.

The questionnaire is widely used by clinical staff in addiction services. I use it as part of the assessment process when I see a new client. The PDF explains how it works. I hope you find it useful.

## 1. Making a Decision

Sometimes you might feel that there are two voices in your head, and these voices are having a constant argument. One is saying that you really should change your drinking; there is an urgent need. The other voice is reassuring you that despite obvious evidence to the contrary, despite your life starting to come apart at the seams, you can carry on drinking. It is saying things like: "Well, maybe I don't have a problem. I don't need to worry. Maybe, I can just leave it as it is." But before you leave it, ask yourself a few questions to diagnose whether you really have a problem.

Here are a few common pointers that alcohol might be a problem. Do any of the following sound like you?

**Do you plan your day around your drinking?**

If you work, do you go to the bar as soon as the workday is done? Or do you open a bottle as soon as you get in the house? Do you find reasons to fit in a little drink during the day? If you are not working, are you looking at your watch, trying to decide when would be a decent hour to have your first drink? If you are going to eat with family or colleagues, do you suggest places where you can be sure of getting a drink?

**Do you know all the best places to get a drink?**

If you are buying a bottle on the way home, do you have an encyclopaedic knowledge of all the places that sell your favourite brand? Do you know how much it costs in different stores? If you like a cold drink such as beer or white wine, do you know which stores keep your brand chilled, so you don't have to waste time chilling your drink when you get home? Do you know all the places that have Happy Hours? Do you know the bars where the owner is most likely to offer you a free drink on the house?

**Does a delay in getting your first drink of the day put you in a panic?**

Be honest with yourself. Do you start to feel a rising tide of panic when something happens to threaten your regular drink? Maybe you need to work late, but all you can think about is when you will be able to get your usual drink. Maybe a family commitment comes up and you are expected to be somewhere, smiling for the family photos, but in your head, you are desperately trying to figure out how you can excuse yourself and get to that drink.

## Are your friends mostly drinking buddies?

You tell your family what great friends you have. They are always there for you – at the bar. You regard non-drinkers with deep suspicion. Even some of your friends irritate you if they don't drink fast enough. In fact, you are the fastest drinker in your group. You find excuses to squeeze in extra drinks.

You pride yourself on your reputation for always being the first to arrive and the last to leave. You boast about having a high tolerance for alcohol. You joke that vodka and orange is a health drink. You love telling drinking stories.

## Do you drink to escape problems?

Whenever life throws difficulty at you, then you drink. You say drink is your friend. Without it, you would be miserable, you tell anyone who will lend you a sympathetic ear. Just look at the bills you have to pay, you say, ignoring the thousands you spend every year on booze. Look at your health problems – another reason to reach for a drink. You can't get a decent job, and your boss is complaining about all the days you have off with mysterious stomach complaints. In fact, life is just so unfair, you deserve to have a little drink, you say.

If that wasn't bad enough, then there are the miserable people in your family who say that if you didn't drink, then your health would improve. You would have the money to pay your bills and you wouldn't have to buy the weekly groceries on a credit card. You would be better thought of at your job. What do they know? They don't understand how tough it is being you.

**Does your drinking embarrass you?**

You're worried that the guys who collect your recycling think that you're an alcoholic because of how many empties you have every week, so you sneak a few bottles into your neighbour's recycling at night when no one's looking.

When you go to the supermarket to buy booze, you buy a bag of salad as well as the litre of vodka so the woman on the checkout won't think you're an alcoholic. Also, you don't buy alcohol from the same store two days in a row, as you are worried that the personnel talk about the amount of booze that you buy.

When you are awake half the night throwing up, you try to convince your partner it must have been because of something not cooked right in your dinner earlier. It couldn't have been anything to do with all the wine you drank, you say, because it was a good vintage.

When the doctor asks you how much you drink, you cringe and lie outrageously. You don't want to get a lecture on how drink damages your health because deep down you fear what you are doing to your body.

**Do you drink when you don't want to?**

Sometimes it seems too much like hard work, but you go for a drink anyway. You don't really feel like it, but you know you have to. You tolerate having to listen to your drinking friends telling the same old boring stories over and over again just because you haven't drunk enough yet. Sometimes you drink when you are unwell. You still manage to get to the store, even though you feel like you are dying.

**Have you tried to moderate or stop your drinking but found it too hard?**

You have woken up a hundred times, swearing that you will do something about your drinking. Usually, your resolve is short-lived and by evening you have completely forgotten and are back at the booze. Maybe now and again you have managed a few days without a drink, maybe even a dry January. But as soon as you started again, it was like a dam bursting. You might have even gone to an AA meeting or two, but then convinced yourself that they are a bunch of cranks and it was not for you.

**Do you wake up in fear of what you might have done the night before?**

Some mornings you wake up in a sweat, reaching for your mobile phone, worried you have sent someone an inappropriate text or sent your boss an email saying what you really think about his management skills. Worse, you worry you might have been in a fight or driven your car to get a take-away while you were blind drunk.

**Do you blame other people for your drinking?**

When you drink heavily because someone has upset you, you believe it is their fault that you drank. You believe that your driving ban was the police's fault – they should have been busy catching crooks, not good citizens like you who had just had one too many.

When you drink because something goes wrong in your life, you believe it is the fault of life, or fate, or the universe that you drank. You believe that you drink because life is unfair, other people are unfair, and that you just need a lucky break in your life, then things would be OK, and you wouldn't need a drink.

If any of these questions sound familiar, then now is the right time to make a decision. In the past, you might have decided to do something about your drinking many times and then a few hours later your commitment has drifted off like so much confetti in the wind. It is easy to at decide four o'clock in the morning when you are hugging the toilet and feeling like you are dying after a big night on the booze, but then later in the day to have forgotten all about that decision.

So, this decision needs to be like no other. It is a commitment to embrace change. This goes against the instinct of an addicted person. Addiction wants to keep you in the same self-destructive loop, day after day, year after year, until it destroys you. That is what addictions do.

Usually, the drinkers I work with have very entrenched routines. Frequently, they are daily drinkers who often start drinking at the same time of the day with such regularity that you could set your watch by them. Then there are the binge drinkers, who usually have entrenched routines but over longer time frames. (We will be talking more about this in the chapter about withdrawal cycles.)

Even when drinkers realize what is happening, they find it hard to go against their instinct and break out of the loop. Sometimes I hear clients saying they can't get out of their "comfort zone", but it is not comfortable at all. It is painful. It is a "discomfort zone". There is nothing comfortable about having your career destroyed by drinking. There is nothing comfortable about being told you have liver disease. There is nothing comfortable about your partner leaving you because you fall into bed every night in a sweaty, drunken heap. There is nothing comfortable about being worried sick about the debts that are piling up. There is nothing comfortable about becoming incontinent. There is nothing comfortable about waking up in a hospital or police cell, not knowing what happened. Yet the discomfort zone drags people back with a magnetic force.

Until they decide to embrace change.

I want you to make that decision now. Don't worry about how you are going to do it because that's what the rest of this book is about. But if you feel ready to make that decision, there is something I would like you to do to mark the occasion. I want you to take a small action because decision without action goes nowhere. You have fallen into this trap before. You have decided to do something about your drinking but ended up drinking again within hours because the decision wasn't backed up by action.

I want you to tell someone important in your life that you have made this decision. Say that you have decided to get a grip on your drinking, and this time you are going to give it everything you've got. Say you're not sure how you are going to do it yet, but you have a book written by a professional to guide you, and you are going to follow it.

You don't have to stop at telling just one person. Tell more. Tell the world. Research shows that people who make a public pronouncement of their intention are vastly more likely to succeed than people who keep it to themselves.

Does that make you feel anxious? That's okay because embracing change will make you feel anxious at first. But it's also exciting. Think about it: anxiety and excitement are quite similar feelings, are they not? And when you have done it, you will feel good.

Do you remember at the start of this chapter we were talking about those two voices arguing in your head? Well, after you read the last couple of paragraphs, I expect the argument erupted again. One voice will be telling you that what I am saying makes sense. That is the voice that wants the best for you, the one that wants you to have a healthier, richer and happier life. The other voice, the one telling you to ignore what you are reading and stay in your discomfort zone, is the voice of your addiction, which is starting to panic because it feels under threat. And you now know what addictions want to do – they want to destroy you.

You don't need me to tell you which voice to listen to. It's time to make that decision.

## 2. Seeing Through the Alcohol Scam

I was recently sitting in a hotel restaurant waiting for my meal, and my attention began to drift to the other guests. The wine waiter was busy attending to his clients. I watched the same ritual as he moved from table to table. He would pour a little wine into a glass for the guest to taste and then stand motionless displaying the bottle's label towards the guest. After swishing around the wine and trying to look like a connoisseur, the guest would then nod, and the wine waiter would fill the glasses of the guests on the table. The waiter then moved on to the next table, where the same ritual would play out.

I wondered how many times that same ritual was happening at dinner tables around the world that evening – probably millions. I've taken part in that ritual myself, and if other people want to drink, that's up to them. But I'm happy not to be involved in the silly wine ritual anymore.

Frankly, I used to find it embarrassing. I would swish the wine around and try to look like I knew something about it, and then accept the bottle. I had a tacit agreement with the wine waiters of the world: I always knew I would accept the wine and they always knew I would too. I was a compliant customer who would willingly pay three times the price that the same bottle would cost in a supermarket and then pretend I knew something about wine. How crazy is that? Sometimes, to break this deadlock and make myself feel better about it, I fantasized about the idea of spitting the wine out in a disgusted fashion and sending the bottle back, just for the hell of it, but I never did.

I used to know a man who owned a vineyard in the Borba region of Portugal, where wine production is an important part of the local economy. I was invited to visit, which I did. It was impressive. The place was a model of shining high tech manufacturing, a finely-tuned machine for churning out the Borba region's wine to the consumer.

The owner proudly presented me with a selection of the wine, including a few bottles of the "good stuff", the expensive wine that the Portuguese who picked the grapes would probably not be able to afford to buy themselves. I tried some of this wine when I got home. I didn't like it. I tried a bit more, thinking I must be missing something. I had seen since I was a child all those food and drink programs on TV where wine buffs droned on about wine being witty, elegant, cheeky, complex, and so on. But I didn't seem to have that ability. I thought there was something wrong with me.

I consulted a friend who had a reputation for being a wine-lover. He was the sort of guy who would drive across a continent just to visit a vineyard with a good reputation. I explained my predicament. I told him that I had been given some good wine, but I just didn't know whether it was witty, elegant, cheeky, or complex. He gave me the sort of superior but understanding look that my old Latin teacher used to give me when I confessed to being completely baffled.

He told me that he knew the wine I was talking about and that it was excellent. The problem wasn't the wine, it was me. I had drunk too much plonk. My palate needed educating. The remedy was for me to study wine, spend huge amounts of money on expensive vintages, and then one day I too would be able to stick my nose knowingly into one of those huge glistening wine glasses and confidently give my verdict on the witty, elegant, cheeky, or complex conundrum.

This illustrates something that sets alcohol apart from other drugs. I have worked with users of many drugs, from tobacco to cocaine to heroin, and most of them realize that they are using a harmful substance. They understand that they are in the grip of a nasty drug that could kill them. I've worked in the needle exchange at a drug project where heroin users would come in to get clean needles and dispose of their old equipment. I've talked to hundreds of users, and I have never met one who glamourized their heroin use. They knew heroin was bad news. Similarly, crack cocaine users know that the drug is bad, even if they love it. Tobacco smokers mostly want to stop. Research shows that 40% of smokers try to stop every year. They know it's a bad drug. If someone gives up one of these drugs, they are usually congratulated, even by people who continue to use the same drug.

With alcohol, however, it's completely different. As my story about the wine illustrates, alcohol is beyond reproach and seemingly it was me that was the problem. I wasn't trying hard enough to understand wine! Alcohol is never to blame. You are to blame.

And because alcohol has this exalted status, if you have a problem with alcohol because you drink too much and it damages your life, then society believes that it is you that is the problem, not the drug.

Surely this cannot be right.

Why does alcohol have this special place among drugs? I know when I gave up tobacco, people said well done, including other smokers because they too would like to quit. But if you tell people you have given up drinking, you are challenged. People want to know why, or they try to break your resolve by cajoling you into having a drink. People assume there is something wrong with you because you have decided not to use the most socially destructive drug on the planet.

One reason for this is that in the western world drinkers are in the majority, and what the majority do is considered normal. Therefore, if you stop drinking you must be abnormal. But that doesn't mean you are wrong.

I was congratulated on giving up smoking, but if I had given up smoking back in the 1950s when 80% of the population smoked, it would have been different. Back then, smoking was considered normal. Nowadays, if you light up a cigarette in the office, you would probably be fired. But back then, offices were full of smoke and employers had an obligation to provide ashtrays for staff and let them smoke all they wanted. Doctors prescribed cigarettes for stress, and indeed in the United States, doctors endorsed tobacco advertising. If I had given up smoking back then, I would in all likelihood have been regarded as odd, just as someone who stops drinking might be nowadays. But that doesn't mean I would have been wrong to stop smoking. As history has shown, I would have been right.

But with alcohol, use is hyped up and glamourized, and we believe the hype and the glamour. From early childhood, we are indoctrinated into the idea that alcohol is good. When I was small, my father worked as a manager for a transport company. At Christmas, the salespeople from truck companies would visit him and give him presents to try to buy his favour. Frequently the gift would be alcohol. I remember him coming home with presentation boxes of wine. It sent to me the clear message that if you wanted to please someone, you gave them alcohol. Therefore, alcohol must be a good thing.

Even from an early age, I was aware of glitzy and persuasive advertising for alcohol. I was invited to "try a taste of Martini, the most beautiful drink in the world" according to the song on the TV ad. "Guinness is good for you," I was told by the ad agency.

Successful people all seemed to drink. As a small boy watching those glittering shows from Hollywood on TV, I thought Frank Sinatra and Dean Martin seemed to float through life on a sea of Bourbon. I didn't know what Bourbon was, but it seemed to be the thing to drink if you wanted a Hollywood lifestyle. And if my father took me to the cinema, I would see James Bond drinking vodka before saving the world and winning over the attractive woman.

No wonder people of my generation grew up with a positive image of alcohol.

It is still the case nowadays that the information we see in the media is heavily biased towards making profits, not promoting healthcare. Mind-numbing sums of money are spent every year on promoting the sale of alcohol compared to what is spent on educating people about alcohol. For example, in 2020, the London-based drinks company Diageo had an eye-watering marketing budget of 1.84 billion Pounds, about 2.4 billion U.S. Dollars. And that's just one company.

With access to these immense marketing budgets, the drinks companies sell us a fictional image of what drinking is like. The image is one of style, sophistication, relaxation, reward, of being among smiling friends, of ideal summers with a cool beer, and perfect Christmases with a glass of port.

The drinker is happy to buy these images as it affirms your drinking, validating your addiction. Alcohol companies don't tell you that buying their brand puts you at risk of permanent brain damage, life-threatening seizures, cancers, stroke and heart attack.

Drink companies trade in human misery. Take, for example, manufacturing beer and cider with 9% alcohol content. The only people who will buy beer that strong will be drinkers who have lost control; only someone with an addiction would want to drink that. The brewers must realize that the market for such drinks is made up of drinkers in crisis. They are cynically pedalling this stuff to vulnerable people who are hopelessly in alcohol's grip, whose health is being seriously damaged.

Likewise, supermarkets that pile up drink promotions right at the entrance of the store, where you have to go past rows of bottles to get to the things you came in to buy. What the retailer wants is for you to make an impulse buy, and this preys on the drinkers who have a problem. In the past, there would be a drinks section that you could avoid. Now drink pops up everywhere. I recently found a random beer promotion in the stationery section of a supermarket. You could go in for a pencil and come out with a pack of Budweiser instead!

It's you, the drinker, who is the target of this marketing. Forget the image of the cosy drinks company that's your friend. It's just not true. All they want is your dollar (or pound or euro or rupee). If you can see through this and see that you are just being exploited, you can use this to start building some motivation. Get angry with these companies for what they have done to you. Some clients I have worked with have found a lot of motivation in getting angry when they realize that the big drinks companies are just using them as pawns, that shareholders profits are valid reasons to destroy people's lives.

I also want you to get past the idea that there is something wrong with you if you cut down or stop drinking. There is nothing wrong with being sober. It's actually rather pleasant waking up feeling happy and well and looking forward to your day, rather than waking up feeling like a freight train ran over you in the night. True, your drinking buddies wouldn't agree, but that's why they're your drinking buddies.

Attitudes are starting to change now. In many countries, we are starting to see health information on adverts and on cans and bottles. Admittedly, it's a bit lame at the moment. In the UK, we are encouraged to "Drink Responsibly". Frankly, that isn't going to make someone who is drinking a litre of vodka a day suddenly cut back. But it is a sign of things to come. Pressure is growing for better health warnings, and maybe eventually a move to plain packaging, as we have seen with tobacco in some countries.

While the majority of people drink, it will take time for this to happen. In all probability, many people in government who can make these decisions are drinkers themselves, so they are hardly likely to be motivated to push for change. But once drinkers become the minority, change will happen much quicker. And this could be on the way. In the United States in 2018, only 55.5% of people reported they drank within the last month, just a small majority.

Increasingly, we see publicity for having sober breaks. Dry January has been around a long time. Sober October has become popular too. More and more we see people taking time off from alcohol, and as this increasingly happens, it will become quite socially normal not to drink. This seems to be particularly taking hold of young people. The Office of National Statistics in the UK reports that one person in five between the ages of 16-24 is teetotal.

Many people simply need advice and information about alcohol. Drinkers usually know surprisingly little about what they're drinking. Sure, they might know the best place in town to buy a Cabernet Sauvignon at a discount, or which store always keeps their favourite brand of beer in the chiller, but they don't know much about how alcohol works and what it does to their minds and bodies. Few drinkers know how to come off alcohol safely.

This book is about to transform what you know about alcohol and how to moderate or stop drinking. I am not going to lecture you and tell you what to do. But I am going to give you the knowledge you need to be able to take a more informed, adult decision about your drinking. You are about to break alcohol's hold over you.

**Free Audio Support.**

To help ensure your success, we at WinsPress.com have created a series of podcasts: ***The Alcohol Recovery Show***. New podcasts go online weekly. I strongly advise you to use this free service – the podcasts will continue to support you long after you have finished this book.

To listen to the podcast, simply go to **winspress.com/podcast**. *The Alcohol Recovery Show* can also be found on major podcast platforms, including Apple, Google, and Spotify.

To ensure you know when a new podcast is available, please join my email service at subscribepage.com/emailservice. (This is a confidential service. You can unsubscribe anytime, and your email will not be given to anyone else.)

# 3. Understanding Alcohol Use Disorder

Alcohol Use Disorder, which healthcare professionals use in assessments, gives us a range to assess the extent of problematic alcohol use in different people, a spectrum of drinking severity. This is very helpful because drinkers are not all the same. What defines heavy drinking will vary from one person to another, and what defines a problem will vary depending on the type of damage that drinking is doing to a person's life.

Physiologically we are all different and the way our bodies process alcohol varies greatly. I have worked with drinkers who can drink relatively large amounts of alcohol without much downside and stop whenever they like. At the other extreme, I had one client once whose problem drinking level was just two glasses of wine – a quantity that most drinkers reading this book would regard as trivial – but because of the inefficient way her body processed alcohol, those two glasses of wine were enough to get her very drunk and give her a three-day hangover.

In this chapter, you will be able to self-diagnose Alcohol Use Disorder. There is no shame in getting a positive diagnosis. Alcohol Use Disorder can strike anyone, regardless of age, race, upbringing, education or genetics. And it's very widespread. According to the American government agency the National Institute of Alcohol Abuse and Alcoholism, 14.4 million adults in the United States had Alcohol Use Disorder in 2018 alone.

I find that talking about Alcohol Use Disorder is more helpful than talking about alcoholism. There are good reasons for this. Firstly, calling someone an alcoholic has very negative connotations, as it is most often used as an insult. It's an unhelpful label to put on someone and it's also a sticky label that people find hard to lose once it has been put on them. If you call a child an idiot, there is a danger that she will grow up believing that to be true and she will underachieve as a result. Similarly, if you call someone an alcoholic there's a danger that he will then start acting out in the way he believes an alcoholic would, and it will become self-fulfilling.

Secondly, using the word alcoholic is very black and white and gives rise to the idea that you are either an alcoholic or you are not. A lot of people believe that if you are an alcoholic, you must stop drinking, whereas if you are not an alcoholic, it's okay to drink. As a result of this, there are a lot of drinkers out there drinking dangerously high amounts of alcohol, but think it's okay because they believe they are not alcoholic. There are also a lot of drinkers who have been driving themselves crazy for years because they have a constant debate going on in their head about whether they are alcoholic, which gets them nowhere.

Alcohol Use Disorder has different categories: mild, moderate and severe. It's really useful in my job for me to understand which category a client falls into because the sort of advice I might give to someone with severe Alcohol Use Disorder would be inappropriate for someone with mild Alcohol Use Disorder. It helps us to be able to treat drinkers as individuals. It gets us away from using a one-size-fits-all approach to excessive drinking.

From your point of view being a drinker, it is also useful because it gives you a realistic idea of where you are in terms of the severity of your problem. It is common amongst drinkers that they are unrealistically optimistic in terms of how well they are doing, or sometimes they might be unrealistically gloomy.

What's more, Alcohol Use Disorder opens the door for making progress. Because in diagnosing Alcohol Use Disorder we look at drinking in the last 12 months, it is not a fixed diagnosis forever and a day. If you are diagnosed as having severe Alcohol Use Disorder, for example, that doesn't mean you will always have severe Alcohol Use Disorder. Over time, as your drinking patterns change, the severity of your diagnosis can change.

I don't want to give rise to false hope that if you have severe Alcohol Use Disorder that you can somehow suddenly and miraculously become a moderate drinker. But you can, with professional help, lessen the severity and make your drinking issues much more manageable.

You can self-assess whether you have Alcohol Use Disorder very simply. In fact, let's do it now. I am going to ask you 11 questions, which come from the National Institute of Alcohol Abuse and Alcoholism. For each question, I want you to answer yes or no.

Here are the questions.

1. In the past year have you had times when you ended up drinking more, or longer than you intended?

2. In the past year have you more than once wanted to cut down or stop drinking, or tried to, but couldn't?

3. In the past year have you spent a lot of time drinking? Or being sick or getting over the after-effects?

4. In the past year have you experienced craving – a strong need, or urge, to drink?

5. In the past year have you found that drinking – or being sick from drinking – often interfered with taking care of your home or family? Or caused job troubles? Or school problems?

6. In the past year have you continued to drink even though it was causing trouble with your family or friends?

7. In the past year have you given up or cut back on activities that were important to you, or gave you pleasure, in order to drink?

8. In the past year have you more than once gotten into situations while or after drinking that increased your chances of getting hurt (such as driving, swimming, using machinery, walking in a dangerous area, or having unsafe sex)?

9. In the past year have you continued to drink even though it was making you feel depressed or anxious or adding to another health problem? Or after having had a memory blackout?

10. In the past year have you had to drink much more than you once did to get the effect you want? Or found that your usual number of drinks had much less effect than before?

11. In the past year have you found that when the effects of alcohol were wearing off, you had withdrawal symptoms, such as trouble sleeping, shakiness, irritability, anxiety, depression, restlessness, nausea, or sweating? Or sensed things that were not there?

You need to answer yes to at least two of the above questions for an assessment of Alcohol Use Disorder.

If you have answered yes to two or three questions, your assessment is mild.

If you have answered yes to four or five questions, your assessment is moderate.

If you have answered yes to six or more questions, your assessment is severe.

I would like to highlight that this is not a diagnosis that is written in stone for all time. Understanding where you are at this moment with Alcohol Use Disorder gives you a starting point. Reading and implementing the information in this book will be a great way to improve your Alcohol Use Disorder assessment.

# 4. Exploding the Myths of Drinking

You will remember in an earlier chapter, we were talking about those voices in your head arguing. Well, before we go any further, I think it's time to disarm the voice of your addiction. As you read this book, that voice is going to do a lot of shouting because it feels under threat. It won't be happy until you are back in the discomfort zone that will destroy you. The main weapon that voice has is repeating myths around alcohol until you believe them. So, let's look at some of these ideas and see if they are really true or simply myths.

**Myth 1: Life would be boring without a drink.**

In the workshops I run with drinkers, this is probably the problem that people raise the most, the question of boredom. People just cannot imagine getting through an evening without a drink. Life would just be so boring. Is this really true?

The following is an extract from a conversation I had with a client called Kevin. Kevin had been doing well and reported how happy his partner was that he had stopped drinking in the evenings.

"It's all been going really great with keeping off the booze," he reported cheerfully. "But obviously, I am going to have a few drinks on Sunday."

To me, this was not obvious at all, but Kevin went on to explain: "It's the football. My team is playing. It's a big game. I'm going to watch it on satellite, on the big screen. It'll be great, I can't wait. Obviously, I'll have a drink." I pressed him further on this as it was still not 'obvious' to me why he would want to undo all his progress by drinking on Sunday.

With a look of total surprise that he needed to explain, he continued: "Well, it would be boring without a drink. Obviously!"

I responded by summarizing what I had understood him to say: "Your favourite team is playing?" Kevin nodded. I carried on: "It's a big game?" Again Kevin indicated I was correct with a cheerful nod. I ploughed on with my next question. "You've got a big satellite TV to watch it on?" Kevin responded with an affirmative. I paused and looked at him with a quizzical expression. "But you would find all that boring without a drink. Is that correct?"

Kevin hesitated "Yes. Well, no. I'm not sure now. Maybe."

I pressed on with my next questions: "You find football boring without a drink?"

"No, I love it." Kevin exclaimed with indignation.

I looked at Kevin pointedly and asked: "If you love it, why do you need the drink?"

Kevin considered this for a few seconds and responded with: "I suppose I've always had a drink when I watch football. I suppose it's just a habit."

I gave Kevin a few seconds to reflect on his answer and then I asked: "So watching the football wouldn't be boring without a drink, then?"

After another pause to reflect, he said: "Now that I think about it, I suppose it wouldn't be boring. And my partner would be pleased. As I think about it, the last time there was a big game on TV, I had a few too many and fell asleep on the sofa. She had spent ages getting Sunday dinner ready and she was really angry. We had a hell of an argument after. Perhaps it would be better just to get some Pepsi in the fridge this time."

You can see what happened here. Kevin had simply assumed that watching the football without a drink would be boring because it was his habit to drink while watching the game, nothing more. It was just a myth that had grown up in his mind. All it took to dispel this myth was to question whether it was really true. If Kevin had concluded that football really would be boring without a drink, then he would have been better finding a new sport to follow rather than getting drunk.

It's not surprising that if you have been turning to alcohol as your go-to action in most situations, you would think that life without it is boring. But next time you are in that situation, consider whether it is lack of alcohol that is boring or is it what you are doing? Should you be looking to replace the activity with something more entertaining or absorbing rather than simply reaching for the bottle?

It is also the case that there is nothing intrinsically exciting about alcohol. If you are sitting alone, doing nothing and bored, all that will happen if you drink is that you will be sitting alone, doing nothing, bored and drunk – hardly a great improvement.

In complete contrast to the drinker who thinks that being sober is unremittingly boring, people who are habitually sober regard drinking as boring. You can see what they mean if you go to a bar and listen to drunken people talking to each other. Short-term memory becomes affected very quickly when people drink, with the result that people keep repeating themselves, and usually louder as well. Not great entertainment.

I run workshops on boredom. I brainstorm with a group of drinkers, who think that life without drinking is boring, all the things they could do without having a drink. On one occasion, the group came up with over 200 ideas in a few minutes. Not bad going for a group of people who said they couldn't think of anything to do! Try it yourself next time you are bored. See how close you can get to our 200, then pick one from your list and go do it.

**Myth 2: Alcohol helps me deal with anxiety and depression.**

This is a widely held belief, certainly among people who come to me for help. I would estimate that 80% of drinkers I see are on prescription anti-depressants when they first arrive for treatment and think that alcohol helps them with anxiety and depression. The irony is that alcohol makes anxiety worse and is a depressant. Using it to combat these things is like putting gasoline on a fire in the hope of putting it out. So why is it that most people don't realize that?

I think it is because the first thing alcohol depresses when it goes into the brain is our self-control, we feel like a dog let off the leash, it's exciting, which gives the illusion that alcohol is giving us a lift. However, it's very short-lived. After a couple more drinks, your mood will be on the way down. But as your memory will be starting to fail, the following day you are much more likely to remember the pleasant bit at the beginning rather than the nasty stuff that happened later in the night.

It is a characteristic of all drugs – whether you are talking about crack cocaine, nicotine, heroin, ecstasy, or alcohol – that it tends to be the bit at the beginning that is the good part. Also with alcohol, you might not realize it, but if it has been a while since you had a drink, you will be in withdrawal. That "I really *need* a drink" feeling is telling you that you are in withdrawal. Consequently, the first drink gives you a lift because that feeling of withdrawal gets washed away, which feels good for a short time.

Heavy alcohol use, in fact, increases the chances of developing depression, increases the severity of symptoms of depression, and makes recovery from depression more difficult. One bit of good news for people suffering from depression and heavy alcohol use, however, is that if alcohol is taken out of the equation, things can improve quickly, with a substantial reduction in depressive symptoms only five weeks after drinking stops, according to National Health Service information.

There are much better ways to deal with anxiety and depression than drinking. Although these conditions are not the topic of this book, the later chapter *Stopping those Spinning Wheels* may be helpful. If anxiety and depression are an issue for you then you might be interested in reading my book '*The Emotional Mind: Overcome Anxiety, Stress, Negativity & Procrastination*'. I can also recommend the book '*Mindfulness for Stress and Anxiety*' by Antonia Ryan. Details of both books are on Winspress.com.

**Myth 3: Alcohol helps me relax.**

Most people, including non-drinkers, would take it as a given that alcohol is relaxing. But is that really true? We are told that alcohol is relaxing and most advertising for alcohol reinforces this idea. You will have seen countless ads showing people enjoying a drink in exotic vacation locations or at the end of the working day with friends. The link between alcohol and relaxation is drummed into us from early childhood, so it's not surprising that when we first pick up a drink, we expect it to relax us.

But is it more the case that drinking alcohol is something we do when we are relaxing already? If you are having a drink after work, you were relaxing already. If you have a drink on vacation, you were relaxing already. And that little lift that alcohol gives you adds to the illusion that it is the alcohol which is responsible for relaxing you, not that you were simply relaxing already.

If alcohol is relaxing, then people would become more relaxed the more they drink. Yet if we look at people's behaviour when they have a lot to drink, we see people getting very excited, upset, crying, getting into fights, domestic violence, and breaking up the city centre on Saturday night. Is that really the behaviour of relaxed people?

One person was referred to me because, after a night of drinking lots of alcohol, he had poured gasoline all over himself and tried to set fire to himself. When I asked him about this, he said he had no recollection of the incident at all and he had no idea why he tried to turn himself into a human torch. Whatever the reason, I doubt it was because he was feeling relaxed.

**Myth 4: Alcohol helps me sleep.**

Here is a short extract from a conversation I had with a client called Bernie. This exchange is typical of the conversations I have had with many drinkers when they have seen me for an assessment:

Bernie was a large, bear-like man in his fifties. He had dark circles under his eyes and a haggard expression. He exclaimed earnestly that he couldn't get to sleep without alcohol. I assessed his eye bags, dull skin and drooping shoulders and confirmed with him: "Alcohol helps you to sleep."

Bernie agreed earnestly "That's absolutely right."

I paused, then asked: "What do you think about when you wake up at 4 a.m.?"

Bernie shrugged his shoulders and responded: "Oh, I just think about what's going on, what I need to do, my mind goes round and round in circles and I can't get back to sleep... Hang on a minute, how did you know I wake up at four in the morning?"

Everyone is amazed that I know they wake up at four in the morning. But it isn't difficult. The majority of daily drinkers wake up around that time.

The reason is the Law of Rebound, which states that every drug has the opposite effect when it wears off. So in the case a stimulant, such as crack cocaine, it makes you energised and happy for a short time when you take it, but the user will be tired and in a low mood for a long time when it wears off. (When it comes to opiates, they make you constipated when you use them, so you had better be near a bathroom when they wear off!)

In the case of alcohol, it wears off pretty quickly. So if you start drinking after work or when the kids go to bed and then alcohol makes you sleepy, overnight it will wear off and around four in the morning your system will wake up, and before you know it, you are wide awake.

**Myth 5: I have a high tolerance for alcohol, so I can get away with it.**

The ability to drink lots is often held up as something to admire. You know the sort of thing:

"He drinks like he's got hollow legs." Or "She can drink all the men under the table". Another common expression is: "He drinks like a fish, but he never seems drunk."

Quite why we have this admiration for people who can drink until they're senseless is hard to say. But it isn't a quality to be admired; it's one to be feared. Developing a high tolerance means is that the body's natural defence system to keep you safe from harm, namely being sick, is bypassed.

If you can drink and drink all night, you are in real danger, as you are able to keep drinking until you reach life-threatening levels of intoxication. You can get brain damage from alcohol-related dehydration, have a seizure as a result of lower blood sugar levels, or have a heart attack or a stroke.

You will be at risk of alcohol poisoning, which is a killer. As we have discussed, alcohol is a depressant, and in alcohol poisoning, the respiratory system becomes so depressed that you simply stop breathing, and then it's game over.

The risk of respiratory failure becomes even higher for people who take medication called benzodiazepines, which includes common prescription drugs like Valium, Librium, Tamazepam and Xanax. Benzos, as they are commonly known, also depress the respiratory system, so if you are taking benzos and drinking, it increases the risk that your breathing could fail.

Ironically, people with high tolerance to alcohol are at risk of developing a condition known as reverse tolerance, which means that tolerance levels drop dramatically. It can happen quickly and the same person who the week before could drink a blue whale under the table suddenly starts getting crazily drunk on tiny amounts of alcohol. What is happening is that the liver has become so damaged that it can no longer process alcohol efficiently, a potentially fatal condition.

**Myth 6: Drinking makes me happy.**

My clients all with have one thing in common when I first meet them, they are all heavy drinkers. Some of them drink astounding amounts of alcohol when they first refer to me.

So, if drinking alcohol makes people happy, then the people I meet in my job would surely be the happiest people in the world, because they drink loads.

But they are not happy – far from it. Most are taking anti-depressants and most have serious life issues, often as a direct result of their drinking. I have also found that the more people drink, the unhappier they are.

This has led me to formulate my First Law of Recovery of Alcohol Addiction:

*"Misery increases in direct proportion to the amount of alcohol taken."*

**MYTH 7: I feel I'm missing out if I don't drink.**

I can't argue with this. If you don't drink, or drink in moderation, you are indeed missing out. Here are some of the things you could potentially be missing out on: hangovers, liver damage, job loss, embarrassing yourself at social events, high blood pressure, anxiety, drunken injuries, debts, memory loss, incontinence, poor eye-sight, arguments with your loved ones, free overnight accommodation in prison, saying things you regret, heavy sweating, jaundice, inappropriate messaging, divorce, blackouts.

Wouldn't you like to miss out on that lot?

# 5. Choosing your Path: Moderation or Sobriety

After dealing with so many drinkers who arrive at my consulting room in search of help, I find it obvious that there are many kinds of drinkers with varying levels of problems. It logically follows, therefore, that there may be various solutions.

Drinkers come in a wide range, the spectrum of alcohol use we saw in chapter three, 'Diagnosing Alcohol Use Disorder'. At one end of the range is the occasional drinker who just has a drink on special occasions and then only a small quantity. At the other extreme is the person who drinks several litres of spirits every day. Everyone else who ever lifts a glass is at some point on the spectrum between those extremes.

There are different theories about where you draw a line across the spectrum and say that those on one side don't have a problem and those on the other side do. In reality, the line is probably fairly wide and vague. This is because what alcohol does in one person's body may be quite different from someone else's. Your size, sex, and age all play a part.

What's more, it's not just the effect on the body that indicates problem levels of drinking. When I am assessing someone who has come to me with drink issues, I will be looking at the effect on relationships, career, finances, criminal record, social standing, self-esteem, mental faculties, happiness and general quality of life. Then I will start putting together a plan with the drinker.

In order to start making a plan to overcome the alcohol issues that have brought you to this book, we will need to consider a fundamental question: which is right for you, moderation or sobriety? To answer this question, take a look at the statements below. Which of these are true for you?

1. If you can't get a drink, you show signs of physical dependence, such as shaking hands, heavy sweating, and feelings of panic.

2. Previous attempts at controlled drinking have quickly ended in failure.

3. You have needed an alcohol detox under medical supervision in the past.

4. You have a strong desire for sobriety or a commitment to AA.

5. There are a lot of heavy drinkers in your family and social group.

6. You have been in hospital because of drinking.

7. You have lost a job because of your drinking.

8. You get verbally abusive or physically violent when drunk.

9. You put yourself at risk when drunk.

10. You have a criminal record because of drinking.

If you answered "yes" to any of the above, I suggest you have an honest heart-to-heart with yourself about whether moderation is really going to work for you. If you answered "yes" to several of the above, then the chances of you sustaining moderation over a period of time are not promising. I am not saying impossible. I have sometimes seen my clients produce surprising results. But I don't want to give you false hope, and I recommend you explore some other options as well, which you will be looking at as you read through this book.

Now take a look at the following list and again consider which are true for you:

1. You have in the recent past had periods of time when you have drunk at non-problem levels.

2. If you were unable to get a drink, it would not cause you any serious distress.

3. You have a strong preference for normal drinking.

4. You have been able to show self-control in other parts of your life, such as giving up smoking, successfully dieting, or having a training program.

5. You are not receiving treatment for serious mental health issues.

6. You do not have addiction problems with other drugs.

7. You get few bad physical reactions to a night's drinking.

8. Drinking doesn't have a detrimental effect on your work.

9. Your family and friends are supportive of your drinking moderately.

10. You are not violent or abusive when you drink.

If you can agree with most of the above 10 statements, then moderate drinking might work for you. That said, just because you can drink moderately doesn't mean you should not become sober. But it does mean you have a choice.

**What research shows us.**

The biggest piece of research on moderate drinking was carried out by William Miller and Ricardo Muñoz in the United States. These eminent professors drew on 30 years of research and clinical trials and published their findings in *'Controlling Your Drinking'*. The results make interesting reading for anyone wanting to moderate.

What the researchers found in their follow up studies was that 15% of participants in the program were drinking at stable levels of moderation, which was defined as 10 American standard drinks per week (equivalent to 17.5 British Units or 14 Australian standard drinks).

Another 23% were described as achieving "pretty good moderation", defined as up to 14 American standard drinks per week (equivalent to 24.5 British Units or 19.6 Australian standard drinks).

In addition, 24% were abstaining from drinking alcohol altogether, while the remaining participants in the program had returned to drinking at harmful levels.

It is encouraging that in total 38% were still drinking at either stable or pretty good moderation. But what I find particularly interesting is the 24% who were abstaining because remember this was a controlled drinking program – people hadn't joined in order to abstain. So why had such a high percentage stopped drinking entirely?

The answer for some people was that as they had been used to drinking to get drunk, they found that moderate drinking seemed pointless, and they might as well not drink at all. For others, they found that moderate drinking was just too hard. Either they simply couldn't do it or couldn't sustain it. They found that not drinking at all was, in fact, easier for them than trying to control it.

Most drinkers when they come for professional help are hoping they can become moderate drinkers. They simply can't face the idea of giving up drinking because it's just too frightening. So people will often say things like: "I'd just like to be able to have a few drinks with my friends at the weekend" or "I'd like to be able to have a drink on special occasions" or "I'd like to be able just to stop after a couple of drinks".

Some drinkers can moderate without too much difficulty and can achieve these aims. Some can moderate, but it's hard work and great effort is required. A significant number, however, are unrealistically optimistic about their ability to moderate and are sadly doomed to failure. If you fall into this last category, you can save yourself time and heartache by facing up to the fact now.

Some people, however, even after a significant period of heavy drinking, can become moderate drinkers. In fact, this is a much more common phenomenon than is often acknowledged. We see it all the time with young people.

There is nothing unusual about single people without responsibilities drinking heavily for several years in their early twenties as part of an alcohol-centred social life. But they don't become dependent, and when life takes a new turn and something more interesting comes along, they simply reduce their drinking or stop.

There is no drama about this. Most of them will not need to enter treatment. All that is happening is that their life priorities have changed and being out with their friends drinking large amounts of alcohol is of no interest anymore.

They have found something more important, more absorbing such as falling in love, starting a family, or launching a career. It doesn't even occur to most of these people that they have escaped the grip of an addictive drug. They just feel that they have moved on.

Another type of drinker I sometimes see in my practice is the person who has been a moderate drinker for years but has suddenly entered a period of heavy drinking and can't seem to get out of it. Usually, we find that there has been a life event that caused this: the loss of a loved one, a relationship breakdown, or the loss of a job are common reasons.

My role is then to provide support until the person has been able to deal with the underlying issue, at which point they can usually make an adult decision about whether to resume moderate drinking or take a break from alcohol.

On the other hand, some people have, by necessity, a very black and white relationship with alcohol. They either drink heavily or not at all. They cannot find a happy middle-ground. They become addicted easily. After perhaps just a few encounters with alcohol in their youth, they become dependent, and there is no such thing as safe drinking for them. In this situation, they may need to go to a medically supported detox, a subject we will be covering later in this book.

Quite why some people become dependent drinkers and others don't is unknown. Some people can give up drinking and go for years without a drink, but it only takes one alcoholic drink for them to become re-addicted all over again. It's instantaneous. Yet other people can drink like a parched horse for years and then suddenly stop with no apparent ill effects, as if nothing had happened.

There are various ideas on why people vary so much in their reaction to alcohol. There are theories around genetics, trauma, and upbringing. But no one really knows. It seems to be an example of human diversity. The important thing for you is to realize which type you are and work from there.

If you are still unsure about which category you fall in to, there is good news. You can defer your choice of path. You can try reducing in stages and see how you feel about it as you go. You might find that it is too difficult. But you might find that you can achieve a plateau at a level of drinking that doesn't cause you problems. Or you might find that you can keep reducing right down to zero.

Later in this book, we will be exploring all this further and constructing your plan for success.

# 6. Choosing Your Method: Reduction or Detox

In this chapter, we will be looking at choosing a method to get to your goal of moderation or sobriety, and I need to make a warning: if you have been drinking heavily, you should not suddenly stop completely. There is a very real danger of seizure. Anyone who has a history of having fits is particularly at risk, but it could happen to anyone. If in any doubt, you should consult a physician.

What happens is that your brain and central nervous system become used to the suppressant effect of alcohol. If the alcohol is suddenly removed, this causes a rebound effect called hyper-excitability, which can trigger a seizure. The risk of seizure should not be taken lightly as it can have very serious consequences.

For this reason, I recommend to clients either to reduce in stages or, if they want to stop drinking completely and find reduction is too difficult, to consider a medically supervised detox. Cessation, suddenly stopping, is something I would only suggest to people who frequently stop already for several days at a time without any sign of withdrawal.

**Reduction.**

You can use reduction as a method whether you want to go for moderation or sobriety, as it's just a question of how far you reduce. With sobriety as a goal, this is simple – your goal is zero. But how about if you want to moderate, what does moderation look like?

Without an international standard, it looks confusing, with different countries giving slightly different recommendations. But to give us a benchmark to work with, let's look at the United States, as this book will probably be read there more than anywhere else.

In the United States, the recommended limit for low-risk drinking is 14 standard drinks per week for men and 7 standard drinks per week for women. That's equivalent in the UK about 24 British units for men and 12 for women, or in Australia that would work out to about 20 Australian standard drinks and 10 for women. You can Google the exact recommendations for your country. In any event, I hope that will give you a guideline to work with for an eventual goal.

I use the phrase "eventual goal" because, if you are drinking five or ten times that amount per week at the moment, these levels of drinking will seem so far below what you are used to that they might well seem ridiculous to you. You probably can't get your head around drinking amounts that seem so vanishingly small.

The solution to this is simply not to worry about it right now – just focus on the first step of a reduction plan. There is no point in obsessing about the later stages of your reduction if you can't achieve the first step.

A good reduction plan would look like this:

1. To begin, you need to know exactly what you are reducing from. What exactly is your starting point? If you are the sort of drinker who drinks the same every day, this is easy. But if your drinking varies, I suggest you download a drinks diary app onto your phone. Choose one that looks fun, as there is no reason why dealing with your alcohol issue should be dreary.

2. Carry on drinking normally for a week. Use your drinks diary app every time you have a drink. You don't need to tell people what you are doing. They will probably assume you are just checking your messages.

3. After the week, work out exactly what your average consumption is.

4. Reduce the amount you drink by 20%, so if for example, you drink 10 beers a day, reduce to eight.

5. Stay at this level for a week, so your system gets used to this being normal consumption for you.

6. After a week, if you are feeling stable, reduce by a further 20% for a week.

7. Repeat until you reach your goal.

So, to sum up, you establish exactly what you are drinking now, and then reduce by 20% per week. Do not exceed the 20% weekly reduction in order to avoid getting an adverse reaction. If at any time you get a bad reaction, such as substantial shaking or hallucinations, get medical assistance. And don't over-think what you're doing, don't start projecting into the future, just focus on this week's goal.

**Detox.**

Now, let's look at the option of detoxing. The word detox gets thrown around in magazines and blogs to describe all sorts of reduction. People talk about detoxing to purge the body of many things. It is also used in a figurative sense. I heard someone talking about detoxing from social media, by which I guess they meant purging your mind.

To detox from alcohol, you need to abstain from drinking long enough for your body to completely purge itself from alcohol. The time varies slightly from person to person, but 10 days should be long enough for most people. If you are not a dependent drinker, you will probably experience some physical cravings at first, but the biggest issue is usually the mind games that coming off alcohol causes. You will find the many techniques discussed in this book will help you. For extra support, I have written another book specifically to counsel people through the detox period, called *"The 10-Day Alcohol Detox Plan"*.

Most drinkers who detox are not dependent and might be abstaining for a short time, like Dry January, or for a specific reason, such as to support a weight loss diet. However, detoxing for heavy drinkers who are dependent on alcohol is a more serious undertaking and should be done with medical support.

Signs of dependency include drinking to stop the shakes in the morning, heavy sweating after drinking, and having the reflex to vomit but with nothing coming up, which is commonly known as the dry heaves. You might feel itchy, like something is crawling across your skin. Hallucinations can occur, especially about insects – you might imagine swarms of wasps are after you.

Drinkers may also need to be detoxed so other medical procedures can be performed. For instance, you might need to have surgery for something unrelated to alcohol, but the hospital will have to detox you to work with you.

Another thing to consider about a medical detox is that it is not a miracle cure. I meet many people in my work who have been through numerous detoxes. It's heart-breaking to see drinkers desperately pinning their hopes on a detox, only to relapse within days. The actual detox itself is just the start. Staying sober afterwards takes dedication. This book will help.

During a medically supervised detox, you will normally be prescribed another drug so your body doesn't go into seizure and you are not plagued by cravings. A drug which is commonly prescribed is chlordiazepoxide, also known as Librium. Your condition will be regularly checked by a nurse, and you will probably be given relapse prevention counselling.

After about a week, you will come off the chlordiazepoxide. You may then be prescribed another drug called acamprosate, also known under the brand name Campral, which you can take for several months to reduce cravings.

Another drug you might come across is called disulfiram, also known as Antabuse. This can be prescribed to people when the initial detox period is over. It works in quite a different way: it's a deterrent. It works by blocking an enzyme in your gut which processes alcohol. The upshot of this is that if you drink with disulfiram in your system, you will probably be very sick.

Disulfiram isn't used much in my part of the world. I don't think medical prescribers are keen to recommend something that can make you sick – it goes against the prescriber's instinct. In fact, I have only worked with one client who used disulfiram. He had been happily sober for over a year but said he liked to take it as a deterrent against him having a sudden moment of madness and picking up a drink. It made him think twice.

Most medically-supervised detoxes are in-patient detoxes in a hospital or private detox facility. However, in some areas home detoxes are available to people who have good support from family at home. A nurse visits every day to check the patient's blood pressure and general well-being. I often attend people on home detoxes to deliver relapse prevention counselling.

You might find that detox in your part of the world is a bit different. If you feel you might need medical support, the first step is to contact your doctor, who can make an appropriate referral.

# 7. Drugs That Can Help: Naltrexone and Nalmefene

In the chapter on detox, we were discussing drugs that are used to help drinkers stop drinking. But what if you don't want to detox? What if you're not even sure if you want to stop drinking entirely?

In this chapter, we are going to take a look at a different type of drug, the opioid antagonist, and in particular two drugs in this class, Naltrexone and Nalmefene. Naltrexone is a generic drug that has been around for decades. Nalmefene is manufactured under the brand name Selincro by the drug company Lundbeck.

The idea of the opioid antagonists is that they block the pleasurable effects of alcohol, so although they don't stop you from having a drink, they take away the desire to carry on drinking. This looks like great news for the drinker who wants to achieve moderation. It also looks like great news for the drinker who wants to stop, as using an opioid antagonist makes it easier for the drinker to reduce safely as a prelude to stopping entirely.

The opioid antagonist works by blocking the receptors in the brain that produce the feeling of well-being and sedation that comes with alcohol, especially that first drink or two. The usual rush of endorphins, the feel-good hormones that alcohol releases in your brain, is effectively switched off. Consequently, the drinker who has taken a drink is less interested in picking up another as the reward system is not active.

One of the main differences between normal drinkers and heavy drinkers is that normal drinkers find that having a drink or two will meet their desire to have a drink – they reach a point where they have simply had enough and want to stop, rather as normal eaters will stop eating when they feel full. But the heavy drinker doesn't have that same sense of having enough, because having a drink, rather than meeting that desire to have a drink, will instead set off a craving for another, which will, in turn, set off a craving for another, and so on until something stops them from drinking or they pass out. However, this should cease to be a problem if using the opioid antagonist.

This way of controlling your drinking was pioneered by Dr John Sinclair, who studied at the University of Cincinnati but went on to practice in Finland. Sinclair believed that drinking to problematic levels was, in fact, a learned behaviour to which some people were more susceptible than others. His research indicated that in certain people the reward, which he called *reinforcement,* was caused by endorphins being released that bind with the opiate receptors in the brain. This sets up a very powerful addictive cycle. His theory was that if you could block the receptors while alcohol was present in the brain, you could break this cycle. The opioid antagonists do this.

He used Naltrexone in experiments with rats while he was still an undergraduate at Cincinnati. Rats were exposed to alcohol over a period of time. Sinclair then took the alcohol away for several weeks so the rats were forced to go cold-turkey. He then re-introduced alcohol to the rats to see if they had lost interest in alcohol during their period of abstinence. On the contrary, he found that they binged when they had the opportunity to drink again. He theorized that alcohol deprivation, rather than reducing the desire to drink, actually increased it. Sinclair went on to confirm his ideas in tests with people. In order to avoid the alcohol-deprivation effect, he used Naltrexone with drinkers to help them reduce and claimed a 78% success rate.

What happens in practice is that the drinker takes the opioid antagonist, Naltrexone or Nalmefene, approximately an hour before drinking. They will then need to do nothing unusual. They are free to drink as normal. There is no need to employ any special moderate drinking techniques.

The drinker should, if the medication works, not drink so much, as the drug is blocking the feeling of reward.

This is then repeated over time. The desire to drink is then reduced a little every time, so this method could work either for someone wanting to moderate or as a slow detox technique for someone who wants to become alcohol-free. Sinclair called this gradual reduction in the desire to drink *extinction*, so the less you drank, the less you wanted to drink, until you didn't want to drink at all. This has become known as the Sinclair Method.

The Sinclair Method has obvious attractions for the drinker. It sounds great. All gain and no pain. You just keep drinking until you naturally lose the desire for it. As Sinclair puts it, you drink yourself sober.

My reaction to the Sinclair method was somewhat sceptical when I first heard of it. Would it actually work in practice? It's one thing for something to have a 78% success rate in clinical trials. It's a little different when you are dealing with real people out in the world.

I have now had the opportunity to work with a number of clients who have been taking an opioid antagonist. In the UK where I work, Nalmefene was introduced by the NHS in 2014. You obtain a prescription from your GP. However, it comes with strings attached: you need to have alcohol counselling alongside taking the drug. That's where people like me come in, providing the counselling.

What I have observed is promising but not conclusive. I stress that I am just talking about my observations of how it has worked with people I have been working with – I have not conducted a scientific study – but the conclusion I am coming to is that Nalmefene can indeed help drinkers. However, it is not a magic solution to everyone's drinking problems, because it seems a lot depends on how the person taking the drug gets on with the side effects.

Some people get along fine with Nalmefene from the start and have no side effects. Others have had side effects the first once or twice they have used it, but it then settled down. Still others have had side effects, in particular dizziness or sickness, which has been sufficiently severe for them to terminate taking the drug.

In those that can tolerate the drug, most report that it does help. I have often heard reports from clients on Nalmefene saying that they have poured a drink, had a few sips, but then forgotten about it, only to notice much later that they still have half their drink left. It also helps if the person has something mentally absorbing to do.

In the case of a client I have been working with recently, he found that his alcohol usage dropped to such trivial amounts that he decided to stop drinking altogether. His GP then changed his prescription from Nalmefene to Acamprosate, a drug that helps to reduce cravings for people who have stopped drinking. You might remember we discussed Acamprosate in Chapter 5.

Interestingly, this client had not started taking Nalmefene with the aim of stopping drinking. He just wanted to cut down. But when his drinking fell to the equivalent of less than a bottle of wine per week, he decided he might as well drop the drink entirely, as he was so close to zero anyway.

His experience shows that Nalmefene can indeed provide a pathway to abstinence if that is what you want. Sinclair's research showed that 25% ended up becoming abstinent of alcohol. The remainder would have to continue taking the drug.

This method gives an extra option for the drinker wanting to moderate or stop. If you think that Nalmefene or Naltrexone could help you, the first step is to talk to your physician, who can then signpost you to a suitable alcohol counsellor to support you.

However, I have found that there is a lack of knowledge among doctors – at least in my part of the world – about using opioid antagonists with drinkers. Surprisingly, it isn't better known, as Sinclair published his "Method for Treating Alcohol-Drinking Response" back in 1989.

If you run into difficulty, there is a non-profit organization that can help. The C3 Foundation was created to promote the Sinclair Method, and they can help in finding a physician in your area who is familiar with the method. They have a website, which includes a link to a TED talk by actor Claudia Christian and more information including a description of the method by Sinclair himself. These resources and more are available on their web site: www.cthreefoundation.org

In the next chapter we will be talking about understanding your withdrawal cycle and how this knowledge can help you better understand your relationship with alcohol.

# 8. Understanding Your Withdrawal Cycle

Understanding your withdrawal cycle can be a key tool in sorting out your drinking difficulties. To explain what a withdrawal cycle is, let's look at a very common scenario, as described by one of my clients, Alex. Here he describes how he became a daily drinker.

**The Daily Drinker.**

Alex said: *"When I first started drinking, it was just on a Saturday night. I had left school and started working, so I had some money in my pocket, and I started going out for a sociable drink. I didn't really think there was anything wrong with it. After all, it was what my friends did, it was normal. In fact, I would have seemed a bit odd if I hadn't gone for a drink. It was fun. I had a laugh with my friends, we played pool, and we tried to pull girls. And we drank. Sometimes we drank a lot. Maybe I would make a bit of an idiot of myself. Maybe I would throw up when I got home. But I didn't think anything of it. I was just behaving like any number of men my age.*

*Pretty soon, the weekend drink started on a Friday night after work and stretched until the early hours of Sunday morning. Again, I didn't think much about this. After all, millions of people have a drink after work on Friday, and lots of them will carry on into the weekend. Why not? You've worked all week – surely you deserve a drink and to relax.*

*No one commented on my behaviour. I was still living at home. My parents didn't drink much, but I know my Dad had been a bit of a boozer when he was younger. So I think they just regarded me as being normal, even on the nights when I got home really steaming drunk.*

*This went on as my weekly ritual for months. Then it changed slightly. I started popping out for a few drinks around Tuesday. It just seemed such a long wait to get to Friday. I didn't drink loads on Tuesdays because I had to get to work the next day.*

*Again no one commented on my behaviour. Why not pop out for a few beers and shoot a few frames of Pool on a Tuesday? I wasn't getting into trouble. There wasn't any harm in it.*

*Then after a while I started to notice something. I began missing alcohol after a couple of days. Waiting three days for Tuesday or Friday to roll around started to seem like quite a pain. For example, at work on Friday morning, I would just be thinking about when I could get out of work and go straight down the pub.*

*So I had a great idea: If waiting three days for a drink was getting hard, why wait? Have a drink before the cravings set in. Brilliant! Problem solved! And so I started drinking every couple of days. Then I found that waiting two days felt too long. So I became a daily drinker.*

*For the next few years, the highlight of my day was getting that first drink immediately after work, and the time frame between drinks got even shorter. I was having a drink at lunchtime, just to keep me going.*

*What followed was years of hell: a broken marriage, heavy debts, a lost driving licence and job losses. I had become – as I heard it described years later at my first AA meeting – a functioning alcoholic. But I wasn't functioning very well."*

What had happened with Alex was that his withdrawal cycle had shortened more and more. To start off, he had a weekly cycle. Then, when he started drinking on Tuesdays, his withdrawal cycle shortened to 72 hours.

This 72-hour withdrawal cycle is common with many drinkers. Often these are people whose drinking doesn't cause many problems. They are drinkers who don't realize they are in a cycle. They would probably be surprised, even outraged, if someone used the word *withdrawal* in connection with their drinking. Drinkers mostly think it is just drug users who experience withdrawal, forgetting that alcohol is a drug, too.

Some drinkers never go past the 72-hour cycle. But for many, it is just a stage on the way to becoming the daily drinker.

Now, let's contrast this to another common kind of drinker: the binge drinker.

**The Binge Drinker.**

In my experience of working with drinkers, daily drinkers greatly outnumber binge drinkers. But the binger's problems are just as valid. At first, it seems that the binge drinker is an exception to the rule of the cyclical drinker. But on closer investigation, the cycle can still be found. It is just a bigger cycle.

A common binger's cycle is where they will drink heavily at the weekend, but then not drink at all in the week. They will say, "I don't have a problem. I can go for days without a drink." They will be convinced that this is true, even if someone looking from the outside can see that their life is falling apart.

However, the reality usually is that they don't drink for several days simply because they feel so hammered from the weekend session that they just can't face a drink. But when, after a few days, they feel better, the urge to drink returns.

Ironically, recovery from feeling sick because of alcohol brings on the urge to drink again, which is guaranteed to lead to feeling sick all over again. It makes no sense that someone would want to behave in this way. After all, if eating peanuts made you feel sick for days, you would simply stop eating peanuts. But when alcohol is involved, common sense goes out of the window.

Another fairly common bingeing scenario is the binger who will drink heavily for a couple of weeks or more, then take at least a week off. This is just an even longer cycle.

A few binge drinkers are impossible to categorize, as their drinking is so unpredictable. In some instances, bingers can even go months between drinks, then for a few days or weeks, they just go off the rails.

I believe that in this last case, what we are seeing are not binge drinkers at all, although they might think they are. They are drinkers going through periods of drinking and sobriety. They don't recognise this to be the case because the period of sobriety isn't intended to be forever.

**Using Your Withdrawal Cycle.**

When you become aware of what your withdrawal cycle is, you can use this information to reduce. What you do is to push the boundaries of the cycle back.

So, let's say for example that you are the sort of daily drinker who always starts drinking after work at 6 p.m. You can push back your starting time to 6.30, stay with that for a few days to get used to it, then move to 7 p.m.

It's important that you don't just drink your normal amount in a shorter time, and don't finish later than normal either. If you keep to this plan, logically you would end up with evenings where you don't drink at all, and then you will be making real progress.

Try adapting this idea to your cycle of drinking. For example, if you are a binger, try taking a day longer than normal between binges, then two days, and so on.

## 9. Using the Power of Time

Here is a story related by a former drinker called Karen. She has now been happily past her alcohol problems for several years. She doesn't struggle with it anymore. She has a very simple attitude to alcohol nowadays. She can take it or leave it, so she just leaves it.

But it hasn't always been this way. She was a heavy daily drinker from her early twenties until giving up over two decades later. Her life had been a mad roller coaster ride of dramatic ups and downs. Finally, she realized that her life was heading into another dramatic downward phase from which she was afraid she might not survive. She realized that drinking had to stop. This is the story of the first few months in her own words:

*"I knew I needed to stop drinking as a matter of urgency. I had all sorts of problems: work, money, relationships, and on top of that my body was giving me a few warnings that I couldn't ignore anymore.*

*I wasn't even enjoying my drinking. It was just a pain. It was something I had to do; it was just pure addiction. I would find myself going out in the rain or snow to get a drink. I knew I would rather be at home in the dry and the warm, but I didn't have a choice. My addiction was demanding that I go out and get a drink.*

*It had to stop.*

*I started by forcing myself to cut down. This wasn't easy. It's amazing how if you just cut down by one drink a day – which doesn't sound like much – just how much you miss even that small amount of alcohol. But I was motivated.*

*Fear of what would happen if I didn't stop was forcing me on. Over a few weeks, I gradually started to cut down. I managed to get down to a bottle of wine a day, or equivalent in other drinks. I hovered around that level for a week. Because I had been used to drinking a lot more than that for years, drinking just a bottle of wine in the evening felt like such a small amount to drink that it didn't hit the spot. The cravings were with me all day long, and that bottle of wine in the evening wasn't satisfying them. It was sending me crazy.*

*Then one morning something fantastic happened, I think that because of all my efforts to cut down, a switch must have just flipped in my head, and out of nowhere I woke and thought to myself: I'm not going to drink today, and I didn't. It felt very weird but okay. I spent much of the day wandering in the countryside, starting to come to terms with my first few hours of sobriety. It felt delicate but good at the same time. That was my first alcohol-free day in years.*

*The following day I woke up feeling okay, somehow cleaner both physically and mentally, and I liked that feeling. But I suddenly realized that I didn't have a plan. I had been so focused on cutting down that I hadn't thought about what I would do when I actually stopped. I started to panic because I didn't know what to do next.*

*I didn't know anything about getting help and what support services were out there. I knew nothing about Cognitive Behavioural Therapy, Mindfulness, government-run drug and alcohol services and other things that people use to help them. But I did have a friend who I knew was in AA. So I asked her if I could go with her to one of her meetings, and that night I toddled off to my first meeting.*

*It was a surreal evening, but that was just because of where my head was. The meeting was nice, the people were friendly, the room was comfy and the biscuits were good, so that ticked a lot of boxes for me. I didn't have much idea what people were talking about. I remember people kept talking about having a program. I had no idea what they meant, but it seemed that having a program was a good thing. I wondered where you could buy one!*

*The first few weeks of my sobriety were, as you can imagine, up and down, but actually not as difficult as I had imagined. I kept going to the AA meetings. I still didn't have much idea what people were talking about, but the great thing was that the meetings were in the evening, and as I used to do my drinking in the evening, it was wonderful to have something to do during my usual drinking hours.*

*My head was still very floaty as I got used to this strange new world. But I was getting to like being sober. It was starting to be fun, which was something I hadn't expected I would say in my last days of drinking.*

*One thing I really enjoyed was driving. I would drive into town at 10 o'clock at night, simply because I could. I wasn't worried about the police, in fact, I wanted to get pulled over and be breath-tested just so I could feel smug.*

*But after about a month of sobriety, things started going downhill. I had heard someone at a meeting say that stopping drinking was like making an emergency stop in a delivery van – it was great to stop, but then everything in the back flies forward and hits you in the back of the head. I started to understand what he meant.*

*That floaty feeling was replaced by a grim realization that dealing with my drinking was only the start. My years of drunkenness had left me with some heavyweight practical issues to deal with which were piling up. As far as the issues that I had brought on myself were concerned, I thought that, well, it was my own fault and I just had to clear up my own mess. But I was also learning that just because you have become sober, life doesn't become fair, and you have to be willing to clear up the unfair stuff as well. The going was getting tough.*

*I was also starting to worry that I had given myself brain damage with my drinking. I remember being at a meeting after about three months of sobriety and feeling the left side of my brain buzzing. I thought 'Oh my God, is it going to be like this for the rest of my life?'*

*On top of this, things weren't going so smoothly with AA. I was still going to the meetings, five or six a week. But I had also started on the 12 Step Program (yes, I had discovered what they meant by having a program) and I was struggling with it. Sure, there was lots of good stuff in it. The lessons I learnt about resentments and self-pity, for example, were great lessons that have benefitted me hugely to this day. But other aspects really didn't sit well with me.*

*I never felt comfortable with being sponsored by another AA member (which is a pre-requisite for doing the Steps). I just couldn't get comfortable with having someone know so much about me whose only qualification for doing the job was being a self-confessed alcoholic. I'm sure the two sponsors I tried were very genuine people, and I am equally sure that there are thousands of wonderful sponsors out there doing fabulous work, but I just couldn't get on with it.*

*During those first six months, I even started to have suicidal thoughts for the first time in my life. This wasn't because of the lack of alcohol. It was because my years of drinking had left me with so many problems.*

*I started to wonder if I had left it too late in life to get sober, that my life was permanently screwed up. It did get easier though.*

*Firstly, I heard people at meetings talk about how they had done AA in their own way and it had been okay. This reassured me that I didn't have to be a 12-Step fundamentalist. I know some people really need to do the AA program rigidly by the letter of the book, and if that's what works for them, I wish them well. But it wasn't my way, and I was relieved to find out that was okay too.*

*Secondly, I started to read up on Cognitive Behavioural Therapy, which I started to find beneficial. It started to answer a lot of questions that I had about my own thinking that the 12 Steps hadn't answered. Also, I had begun trying mindful relaxation, which was starting to help.*

*Then after about six months of sobriety, something really marvellous and unexpected happened. I began experiencing short periods, just a few minutes, at random times without warning, when my head just felt great. I can best describe it as being like when a beam of sunlight breaks through a dark grey sky and lights up the landscape. Then it would go away again. I began looking forward to these random happenings. I had no idea what was going on, but I wasn't complaining.*

*Over the next few weeks, it started happening more often and lasting longer. Then I realized what was happening. My brain was regenerating. I was experiencing what it was like to have a lucid mind for the first time in decades, and it was great!*

*In the years that have followed, I have moved on amazingly in my life. I have studied and forged a new career, which would have been impossible with my old drunken brain. AA, Cognitive Behavioural Therapy and Mindfulness have all played a part. More recently, working with a qualified recovery therapist has helped draw it all together. Alcohol is no longer a big, scary addiction that I don't understand. I don't have to hide from it. I don't care if alcohol is around. It has been put firmly in its place."*

**Taking a sober break.**

We can see from Karen's story what can happen if we just give the brain time to repair itself. In getting into recovery from Alcohol Use Disorder, sometimes the best thing we can do is just relax and let time perform its miracles as the body and mind regenerate.

Alcohol is often associated with liver damage, and for good reason. But whereas liver damage can take a long time to develop and does not affect every drinker, damage to the brain happens much quicker and to some extent affects all heavy drinkers. It shows up in memory loss, moodiness, anxiety, depression, and poor decision making.

In the case of some extreme drinkers, the damage can be permanent. But for most people, the damage can mostly be reversed if the brain is given time without alcohol to repair itself – a sober break.

For this reason, I recommend to drinkers who are seeking moderation rather than abstinence that they too consider taking some time out away from the booze altogether. It gives the brain time to repair itself and crucially it also breaks that addictive cycle.

I have seen many times that drinkers usually fail to achieve moderation without taking a period of total sobriety first. So having a sober break makes sense, even if you are intending to drink again. What's more, if you cannot decide whether to reduce or stop drinking, having a sober break will help you make an informed decision. You already know what drinking is like. If you give sobriety a trial period, you can then compare the two. And who knows, you might like the experience of being sober so much that you might not go back to drinking.

So how long should your sober break last for? Well, there is no maximum time, as long as you like, in fact, the longer the better. You know from Karen's story the benefits really kicked in after six months, and six months is a common period to really start feeling big benefits.

If the idea of going six months without a drink scares you witless, then just pick a shorter time frame, a couple of weeks is better than nothing, and a month is better than a couple of weeks, and so on. When you reach your chosen target, you can then choose whether to extend it or not. My book *'The 10-Day Alcohol Detox Plan'* will help you kick-start a sober break, starting with a target of just 10 days.

It is entirely up to you. No one is taking alcohol away from you. It is not a punishment. Alcohol will still be at the store if you want it. Just remember, however, that when you pick up that drink, you are potentially also picking up the problems that led you to buy this book, all over again.

# 10. Your Timeline for Change

In the past, there were many theories about how people in addiction made changes. But the model that has proved to have stood the test of time, and is now near-universally accepted, is known as the Stages of Change.

This was created by two researchers from the University of Rhode Island – James Prochaska and Carlo di Clemente – who had a great idea. Instead of theorising about how change occurred, they went out and asked lots of people who had actually done it. This was in the 1970s and at that time the dangers of smoking had been known for over a decade, resulting in many people giving up. They interviewed people who had stopped and asked them what had happened. The results of this research were published in 1982.

The Stages of Change has since been found to apply to other addictions, not the least being alcohol, and people like myself who work in the field are all familiar with the theory. It's a cornerstone of modern addiction treatment. I have found that clients have also benefited from understanding the stages of change because it gives them a framework to understand where they are in terms of their recovery. It also helps to give you a timeline to work with, so you can plot your progress.

**Stage One: Pre-contemplation.**

Contemplation means thinking about something. Therefore, someone in pre-contemplation hasn't yet started. They haven't realized that the problem exists. They have no interest in change. The penny has yet to drop.

Drinkers can be in pre-contemplation for years, even though the evidence is stacking up and everyone around them can see quite clearly that the problem is there. One quite remarkable example of someone who had spent years in pre-contemplation, even though alcohol was like a wrecking ball in his life, was Mike. He came to me unwillingly (drinkers in pre-contemplation are always unwilling) sent by family who were concerned he could be facing another term in jail if he didn't stop drinking.

Mike presented as a nice guy in his thirties, a bit confused as to why his family had sent him to talk to me. I invited Mike to tell me about his drinking.

Mike shrugged and replied: "Well, I like a drink. But there's nothing more to it than that."

I pointed out that his family were concerned and seemed to think his drinking was a problem.

Mike conceded that the last time he was arrested, he had had a drink. I asked Mike to tell me what happened.

Mike shifted in his seat and sighed. He went on to explain what had occurred: "I was just down the pub at lunchtime with my brother, and you know how things can get a bit out of hand…."

I encouraged Mike to continue. He carried on: "It was silly really. It was my brother's idea. We decided to go and rob the post office across the road. It wasn't serious. We were only after some beer money."

I asked Mike if he was drunk at the time. Mike laughed as he confirmed he was "Drunk as a skunk!"

I asked Mike how many times he had been to prison. He replied: "Nine times. I'm sick of it. I don't think I'm cut out to be a criminal. I keep getting caught."

I said slowly: "You've been to prison nine times. How many of those times did you go to prison for offences you committed while drunk?"

After a long pause Mike replied "Well, now that you mention it, all of them."

I repeated: "Alcohol has put you in prison nine times?"

After another long pause Mike's expression became more serious and he said: "I see what you're getting at."

That was Mike's moment of insight. In all the times he had been to prison, he had always thought it was his fault because he wasn't cut out to be a criminal. It had genuinely never occurred to him that it was the alcohol all the time. This isn't a judgement on Mike – it is truly amazing how alcohol can blind people to the obvious.

**Stage Two: Contemplation.**

At the contemplation stage, you know there is a problem, but you're struggling to change. This is a painful place to be. I always know when I am talking to someone in contemplation because they tell stories of often daily struggles to manage their problem. They will refer to waking up in the morning, feeling sick and remorseful, not wanting to drink again. But by the evening they are once again roaring drunk. They often don't understand why.

People can spend years in this painful place, knowing that they need to do something, but seemingly incapable of taking any meaningful action. Sometimes they never get out – they die in contemplation.

**Stage Three: Decision.**

Unlike the previous stages, the decision stage can be very quick. Life becomes so painful that a serious decision to change takes place and the drinker is finally propelled forward from the pain of contemplation. A decision can take place suddenly and unexpectedly after a long period of contemplation.

**Stage Four: Preparation.**

Now things are happening. You, the reader of this book, could be in preparation right now. Buying this book is part of your preparation. This stage need not take long, not longer than a month, and maybe only a few hours.

It could involve ringing up your doctor or local drug and alcohol service to make an appointment for an assessment. It could involve you researching when your local AA meetings are on. It could be that you register with a recovery web site, like Smart Recovery, which we'll be discussing later in the book. You are making plans.

**Stage Five: Action.**

This is a very busy time. When you are in the action phase, you are typically going to lots of recovery meetings or spending evenings on recovery web sites. You are reading lots of recovery-based material and learning new skills. You may be signed up to a Cognitive Behavioural Therapy course. You could have enlisted one-to-one support from an addictions therapist like me. You may be in AA and studying the 12 Steps, or you could have discovered Smart Recovery and are doing the 4-Point Program. There is more about AA and Smart later in the book. You are making friends with other people who are doing the same thing.

A typical time frame for this period is 3 to 6 months. As you can see, there are different ways of doing the action phase. The right way is the one that is right for you. If you are still not sure what your plan should be, later chapters in this book will show you a way that works for you.

**Stage Six: Maintenance.**

The action phase is very busy and too busy to sustain over a long period. But after a few months, it should be possible to slow things down a bit and get into the maintenance stage. This stage will see you becoming less obsessed with recovery and getting back into normal life.

If you have been drinking heavily for years, normal life is something that will take some getting used to, so you will still need to be very vigilant for trigger events that could cause you to relapse. You will still be taking an active interest in recovery and still attending meetings, or using online support, and maybe seeing a one-to-one counsellor. But you won't be doing so much and with less intensity. You might have even started doing some mentoring with people who are trying to get into recovery.

The time frame of the maintenance stage is controversial. AA believes that the maintenance stage is for life, as AA theory is that once an alcoholic, always an alcoholic – even if you don't drink anymore and haven't touched a drop for years – so you always need to stay in maintenance and work on your recovery. On the other hand, Smart Recovery believes that after a year or two, you should be ready to get on with normal life and leave recovery. Smart calls this "graduation".

So, which is right? I think that it depends on the person. Some people can indeed just move on, they leave their old behaviour in the past and that's where it stays. But other people cannot do that, and they need to stay vigilant for good. I think a lot depends on how severe their drinking was to start off with and how long they had been drinking at harmful levels.

**Stage Seven: Lapse or relapse.**

This is not strictly a stage, it is an event, and I hope it's an event that you don't have to deal with. But realistically, not everyone gets it right first time. Some people will need to have several attempts to reach their goal. So, what's the difference between lapse and relapse?

I would call a lapse just a quick slip that might only involve one or two unplanned drinks, and which is over in a day or so. It doesn't do much damage to your plan and you can pick up again at the stage you were at before.

A relapse is a full-blown return to your old levels of drinking over a period of several days. This is likely to mean you go back through the stages, quite possibly all the way back to the contemplation stage.

If this does happen, it isn't the end of the world, and all being well, you can learn from what went wrong and quickly get back on track. The important thing is to act quickly. The longer you stay in relapse, the harder it is to get out.

In this next chapter, we will discuss motivation in detail.

## 11. Building Motivation

If you search YouTube for the word motivation, you will see lots of videos of people getting pumped up. If you search Google Images, you will see lots of motivating slogans. And maybe this sort of thing will work for a short time.

If you see a team sport like football, before the game you will often see the players huddled together going through some sort of ritual bonding to help get them motivated for the game. That's great when you just need to get motivated for a short while to play football.

Getting motivated to address an alcohol problem is a different matter. You need to find a different kind of motivation: one that can be sustained, and one that works all round the clock, every day, not just for an hour or two. I often hear clients say they can't get motivated, but then after learning a few simple techniques, they find that they can after all. In fact, anyone can get motivated, it's just a question of how – it's a learned behaviour.

In this chapter, I am going to share with you some motivational techniques that I have seen my clients use time and again. There is nothing complicated about these techniques. There is no need to get into any deep psychology. When it comes to motivation, it's the simple techniques that work the best. So let's look at a few:

**The pros and cons tool**

It's really important to write things down. I know it sounds like a pain. Why should you write things down when they are in your head already? But please trust me on this one – writing things down makes a big difference. And write it big. Make it bold. Put is where you can see it.

A good place to start your writing is with the reasons why you want to control your drinking. Here is a simple way of brainstorming this with yourself. This technique has been used countless times, and it works. Simply take a piece of paper and put a line down the middle. At the top of the first column, write "Advantages of Drinking" and at the top of the second column write "Disadvantages of Drinking".

Now get writing. Your advantages of drinking column might contain things like "I like getting high", "I feel more confident socially" that sort of thing. You decide. It's your life, so write down what is important to you.

In the disadvantages column, you might write things like hangovers, driving bans, arguments with my partner, early death, throat cancer, incontinence, financial worries, weight gain, diabetes, heart attack, all sorts of fun stuff like that. But again, this is your list, put down what is important to you. Take your time about this exercise. Put aside an hour when you will not be disturbed. Get as many thoughts on paper as you can. You might surprise yourself with what comes out of your head.

What you will probably end up with is a short list in the advantages of drinking column and a very long list in the disadvantages of drinking column. I have done this exercise many times with people in workshops. Sometimes we brainstorm a group version on a flipchart. It can be a moment of major insight for people. You might have thought you knew why you want to take action on your drinking but doing this exercise can bring it home.

There's a guy I met called Pete who told me a great story about how he had used just such a list. He said he worked in South America as a surveyor for a multinational company. The area he lived in was pretty remote. There was a small English-speaking ex-pat community and as often seems to be the case in the ex-pat world, alcohol was central to much of the socialising.

Pete realized one day that he had managed to get himself addicted to alcohol. He was having difficulties getting up for work, he was sneaking drinks at lunchtime, he had a couple of warning signs from his body that he might be getting incontinent, he was having embarrassing memory lapses, and most of the time he felt lacking in energy and in a low mood.

In the remote area where he lived, there were no recovery meetings he could attend and no local drug and alcohol services he could access. But he did find some useful advice on the internet including a suggestion to do a pros and cons list as I have recommended here. So he did that.

He looked at it and he found the arguments against drinking compelling. He told me that he framed that piece of paper and put it up on the wall of his bedroom where he would see it every morning when he woke up, and that piece of paper had kept him sober ever since, which is a few years ago now.

Pete's story is a powerful example of how just writing things down can have a big impact. You can also see how powerful your thinking can be when you see it in front of you. No one had told Pete what to put on the paper. No one had tried to persuade him to stop drinking. The simple two-column exercise had been a way for him to download his thoughts on to paper so he could see them.

## Keeping a journal

Another way of finding motivation through writing is by keeping a journal of your recovery from your alcohol issues. You are doing is an amazing thing – it deserves to be recorded. It will be a history of your achievement that you will be able to look back on with pride at a future date.

You can use it to record whatever you want, but here are some suggestions:

Your target in terms of alcohol consumption (or lack of) for the day and what you actually achieved in practice.

Your feelings, whether good or bad or just neutral.

Any trigger events and how you handled them; for example, if a friend unexpectedly turned up at your place with a bottle.

How you slept and how felt when you woke up.

If you are taking a sober break, how many days so far.

How people are reacting to you now and changes in your relationships.

How much money you have saved.

Your hopes for the future.

Your plan to keep you on track for the following day.

List the people you met and whether they were helpful to your aims.

Keep a record of the recovery meetings you attend.

And anything else you find motivating.

I suggest also being creative with how you use your journal. Drinking dulls down your creativity, so crank up your creative side by using colour in your journal – maybe include a few drawings, maybe some mind maps. Let your self-expression free. This will help to keep you sober because the part of your brain you use being creative is a different part to where your addictive urges live. Make it lively, make it fun.

As you get going with your journal and begin recording achievements it becomes self-motivating. You might find, for example, that you can resist that extra drink simply because you want to record in your journal that you hit your target for the day.

**Don't try harder – make a plan.**

I have a pet hate: people saying they are going to *try* to do something, particularly the drinkers I work with. You might think this is odd, you might think I want people to say they are going to try. But I don't. That statement is usually followed by failure. What I want to hear is that they have a plan.

Compare these two conversations:

**Conversation A**

Me: "So how are you going to achieve your alcohol goal this week?"

Larry: "I'm going to try really hard."

**Conversation B**

Me: "So how are you going to achieve your alcohol goal this week?"

Sally: "I have made a plan for where I'm going to be all week. I don't want to have any time where I've got time with nothing to do but think about drinking. I'm going to recovery meetings on alternate nights, and on the other nights, I've arranged to meet non-drinking friends. I want to lose weight, so I am recording my weight every morning as a motivator to keep off the booze because there are so many calories in alcohol. I'm also putting all the money I used to spend on drink in a big jar where I can see the money pile up, and on Saturday I'm going to take some money out and buy myself some new shoes."

Who do you think is likely to succeed? If I was a betting man, my money would be on Sally every time. She has a plan, and plans are motivating.

**Take an action.**

People think that you need to be motivated to get into action. But try it the other way round. Instead of waiting to get motivated, do something, anything, just to get rolling. You will find that your motivation starts to wake up and you get some momentum going. It's really important, though, not to over-think it. If you start to give it too much consideration, prevarication is likely to set in.

A great way to get rolling is to do something in the next 60 seconds. That's too short a time in which to over-think. It's also such a short period that you don't need to think too much about what you are going to do anyway because there isn't that much you can do in 60 seconds.

Here's an example. Let's say you normally start drinking at five o'clock in the afternoon. To break that habit, you've decided that at five you're going to take your dog for a walk instead. Great idea, but when five o'clock rolls around, you look out the window, you think it might rain, you start thinking: perhaps I ought to leave it a few minutes. Then you leave it a few minutes more. Over-thinking has led to prevarication. Before you know it, you've cracked open a beer, and you've lost the game.

Now let's do it with a 60-second action. The same scenario, it's five o'clock, the weather looks a bit dodgy, but instead of thinking about that, you do the 60-second action that you've decided in advance. That 60-second action is simply to put the lead on the dog. Nothing more, you have 60 seconds to put the lead on your dog. In all probability, before you have time to think about it, you and your furry friend are off down the road and you've won the game.

Another example: as part of your efforts to get sober, you've decided to start exercising in the morning. Prioritising looking after yourself is a great way to cut down the importance of alcohol in your life. So you set your alarm for early. When the alarm goes off, your mind starts telling you to roll over for a few more minutes. Next thing you know, you've slept in and lost the game.

Now imagine the same scenario, but this time you've decided your 60-second action is to put the coffee on – nothing more, because you can't do more in 60 seconds. So the alarm goes off, and before your mind can start to convince you to stay in bed, you've got the coffee pot in your hand and you're feeling ready to roll.

**Make a chart.**

This is another idea that is so simple but incredibly effective.

You need two things. A goal to aim for and a wall planner, which you can get from a stationery store, even a big calendar will do.

I can give you an example of how this has worked to crack an addiction in my own life. In my case, it doesn't involve drinking, it involves smoking, but you will easily be able to use the same idea for drinking.

I was a smoker for many years. I was so addicted to nicotine, it was crazy. I had tried all sorts of things to stop – patches, nicotine chewing gum – but nothing worked until I got a calendar with a month displayed on it. I also got a packet of stickers. Some stickers had sunshine symbols on them, and others had rainy symbols on them. I put the chart up on the wall in the kitchen where I would see it numerous times every day.

The strategy was simply this: at the end of the day, if I had not smoked, I would put a sticker on the calendar for that day. If I'd had an easy day without smoking, I would put up a sunny symbol. If it had been a difficult day being without tobacco, I would put up a stormy symbol. But the most important thing was that I was going to get to the end of the day and put up a sticker.

I made this the most important thing in my day. In fact, for a month, it was the most important thing in my life. Come hell or high water, I would get through the day without smoking so I could put up that sticker. If I had to crawl across hot coals to get to the end of the day and put up that sticker, I would do it. No patches, no nicotine gum, and above all no excuses.

By the end of the first week, I had seven stickers up on my chart – and they were all rainy symbols! It had been hell. But I was proud of my achievement. Every time I saw the calendar, which was many times every day, I felt proud and I was motivated even more to keep going. The fact that it had been hell was also motivating – I never wanted to go through that again, so this time had to be it. No turning back.

I got to the end of the month and admired my chart. I didn't carry on with the chart technique after the month, because by then I had cracked it. I think there were three elements in the success of this strategy:

1) It was simple, over-thinking couldn't come into it.

2) I had turned quitting into a game, and games are very motivating.

3) It was very visual. Every time I went into the kitchen, the calendar was in my face.

So use this with your drinking goal. You can use it for days without drinking, or days without going over a moderation level, whatever your goal happens to be.

**Make your autopilot work for you.**

Have you ever been intending to drive somewhere you don't normally go, and suddenly realized that you have instead taken a more familiar route without thinking about it? How did that happen?

Your onboard navigation system has overridden your intended route. I am not talking about the navigation system in your GPS; I am talking about the autopilot in your head.

Every time you took that familiar route in the past, perhaps it was the way you drive to work every day, the neural pathway in your head got more and more entrenched, and unless you are trying to override it, it will take control and take you on the route it thinks you want to go.

Heavy drinkers are usually people with deeply entrenched routines. Take for instance the phenomenon of the most common problem drinker – the daily drinker. The daily routine will usually start with a ritual of getting over the night before. It might include coffee, showering, an emergency trip to the bathroom, trying to get some food inside you. In the case of more dependent drinkers, it might involve having a drink to stop the shakes.

There might also be a mental routine, beating yourself up for getting drunk again, thinking up excuses for why you can't perform your duties like going to work or getting the kids to school, without admitting it's just because you are too hungover. The routine will then follow a familiar pattern that ensures the drinker gets drunk again at some point in the day.

But even entrenched habits can change if you want them to. I have seen instances where this has happened very suddenly, much to the surprise of everyone and especially the drinker concerned. I have seen examples where the drinker has had a sudden deeply moving moment of insight that has completely changed their view of their drinking. This is often triggered by a negative event, such as an arrest, an accident, a doctor's diagnosis or a loved one leaving because of the drinker's level of alcohol use. Or sometimes it might be that one day the drinker just reaches a tipping point: one day they wake up and think, I can't do this anymore, and they never drink again.

Such events are remarkable and inspiring, but they are the minority. I would not advise drinkers to wait for this moment of insight before taking action, as they might die waiting. In the vast majority of cases, it comes down to taking determined action to change the routine. This can take a while, and it might need a few attempts to get it right. But if you can start to flip your negative routine to a positive routine and use the power of habit to work for you instead of against you, this becomes self-motivating. You will want more because success is addictive too.

But how do you perform the miracle of turning around this deeply entrenched habit? Breaking out can seem hopelessly difficult. After all, even changing simple habits like biting your nails takes work. So what hope is there when the problem is compounded by having a hugely addictive substance like alcohol involved?

The answer might lie in the analogy we made earlier with driving and overcoming the autopilot in your head.

Consider this: if you want to take a different route, there might only be one key adjustment you need to make. Perhaps there is just one key road junction where, if you turn left you will find yourself on your usual route and will inevitably end up at your usual destination – namely, being drunk. But if you turn right, you will, with no further effort, find yourself following a whole new route. It all came down to what action you took at that key junction.

Now we can look at that in a real-life example. Let's take the example of a drinker who is out of work and finds himself drinking in the morning, leading to a drunken day and all sorts of self-defeating chaos. The key moment – arriving at that important junction – will arrive early on. It might be, for example, when he decides to go to the local store and get his first drink of the day. So the key to taking a different route and avoiding the day of chaos is in that single moment.

If the drinker can put a different action into his routine at that point and make that the most important action of the day, a totally changed day can flow from there. There can be any number of things he could put in place. There might be a support meeting at his local drug and alcohol service he could go to. He could sign up for Thai Chi at his local leisure centre. There could be a sober friend he could meet for coffee. He could do some voluntary work that would take his attention. There exists any number of things he could do that could transform the route his day takes.

Now take a look at your routine. Is there a critical junction in the day that leads you to a drink? What could you do at that junction to change the direction of your day? For instance if, like most drinkers, you like to have your first drink on an empty stomach, then changing direction could be something as simple as having a sandwich half an hour before your normal drinking time. Now find your junction and decide how you can take a different direction at that moment.

# 12. Crushing Those Cravings

Having a technique to deal with alcohol cravings is a fundamental skill to develop in order to control your drinking. Over the past few years, my clients have tried many techniques and here are a few of the ones that they have found work particularly well. You don't need to use all of them. Just having one that works for you consistently is enough. These are visualization techniques that help demystify alcohol.

**The Screaming Kid.**

Imagine you walk into a supermarket and you see the following scene. There is a two-year-old boy, rolling around the floor, crying and screaming at the top of his voice, face turning bright red. The child has seen a little sugary snack. In the child's mind, this little snack is now the centre of his universe, getting it is all the kid cares about.

Standing by the child is the parent, looking very uncomfortable, concerned for the child but also very embarrassed at what is going on in a public place, with a crowd of onlookers starting to gather. The parent is trying to comfort the child with reassuring stories about having dinner when they get home.

But the kid is having none of it because he wants that snack, nothing else will do, and he wants it now, right now, this very second. He doesn't care about the parent. He doesn't even care about his own safety as he rolls around, banging its fists on the floor, in an uncontrolled fit of self-pity (because he doesn't have what he wants) mixed with outrage (because the parent is not giving him what he wants).

If you were the parent, what you would do?

When I put this question to drinkers who attend my workshops, responses vary. Some say they would give the kid the snack just to get some peace, and then get out of the store as soon as they could.

But most people say they wouldn't give in, because if they were to give in, it would only encourage the child to behave in the same way again in the future, maybe worse. They are right.

Next time you have an alcohol craving, try imagining the craving is that screaming kid. It's all about wanting something right now, to the exclusion of all else, with that same mix of self-pity and outrage because you haven't got a drink. Now imagine that you are the parent (the person trying to control your drinking) looking down on that screaming kid (your craving).

What are you going to do?

You have a choice. On one hand, you could just give in. Give the screaming kid (the craving) what it wants (a drink) to shut it up. The problem with this, however, is that by giving in, you guarantee that the screaming kid (craving) will soon be back, and next time it will be even more demanding because it knows it has the measure of you. What's more, that kid is going to grow up and become an even bigger problem every year.

On the other hand, you can be firm. You will have to tolerate a lot of screaming, but that isn't going to kill you, and in the long run, you will be the responsible parent with a well-behaved child.

**Play the Movie through to the End.**

This technique is a big favourite with many of my clients. It's called 'Play the Movie Through to The End'.

I want you to imagine that the craving for a drink is like a trailer for a movie. Trailers always show the best bits to entice you to go see the whole movie.

In the same way, when you get a craving, your mind plays a "trailer" of how it would like you to believe the experience of having a drink is going to be. For example, it might conjure up an image of you sitting contentedly in a comfortable bar as the waiter pours your favourite drink. Or it might show you an image in your mind of you having a laugh with your friends, with you the centre of attention. Maybe it might even show you a scene of you being witty and attractive to someone you want to impress.

But now play this movie through to the end. How does the movie of you giving in to a craving normally end? What are the final scenes usually like?

Is the final scene usually you having a blistering row with your partner? Or is the final scene you on your knees in the bathroom, your head down the toilet? Or is it the traffic police pulling you over to the side of the road? Or is it you waking up to the realization that you made inappropriate comments to everyone you know on Facebook? Or is it your boss telling you you're fired? Or is it you looking in the mirror and being disgusted by what you see looking back at you in the morning?

When you get a craving, don't just judge it based on the trailer – play the movie to the end.

**The Box of Cravings.**

The next technique is a game. It comes as a surprise to drinkers who attend my workshops that I talk about playing games. Surely, they say, with something as serious as alcohol dependency, you can't play a game with it.

I disagree, and this is why: games are energising, games are motivating. Take for example a teenager who feels that he (it's more likely a boy) is just too tired to get up and can't be bothered to get out of bed. If you are a parent of a teenager, you will know what I mean. But give that same teenager a new game for his console, and that teenager who moments earlier could hardly stay awake will suddenly become totally energized and won't need sleep for days. That's the power of a game.

So this is how we play the game called Box of Cravings:

Imagine there is a box that contains all the cravings you have for alcohol. Standing by the box is your opponent. In this contest, your opponent is your addiction. The idea of the game is that your opponent is going to throw the cravings at you, one by one. What you have to do is to dodge the cravings.

If you let one of the cravings hit you – which happens when you pick up a drink – you lose the game, the box of cravings becomes full again and your opponent is restored to maximum energy. But if you can keep dodging them until the box is empty, you win.

This is a game that gets easier for you the longer you can keep going because the biggest cravings are at the top of the box, and the more the box empties, the more your opponent has to use smaller cravings that are less likely to hit you. Also, your opponent gets weaker as the game goes on and starts throwing the cravings less often and with less force.

This game is a good indication of what happens with cravings in reality. When you first stop taking alcohol or any addictive substance, the cravings will be big, and they will be frequent. But the longer you go on, the easier it gets until eventually, you win.

A nice thing about this game is that you can get to a point where you welcome the cravings because you know each time you have one thrown at you, the box gets a bit emptier and you are closer to victory.

## 13. Winning the Head Game

When it comes to normal drinkers – by which I mean people whose drinking doesn't create problems for them or people around them – you usually find that they drink to enhance good feelings.

For example, this type of drinker will usually drink when they are meeting friends for dinner, having family get-togethers, or to celebrate happy events. In other words, they drink in situations where they will be expecting to enjoy themselves. In these situations, alcohol may indeed work to enhance happy feelings, as this type of drinker doesn't normally drink enough for the bad side of alcohol to kick in.

By contrast, when it comes to problem drinkers – by which I mean people whose drinking creates chaos for them and people around them – you usually find that they drink to escape negative feelings.

For example, this type of drinker will usually drink when they feel offended, when they heard bad news, when someone says something they find objectionable, when they feel life is unfair, or when they feel overwhelmed. They will drink to excess, which brings on the bad side of alcohol and things just spiral down.

An experiment I have often carried out when I have been running meetings for drinkers is to pose this simple question: Why do you drink alcohol?

Having done this several times with dozens of drinkers, I can reveal that nearly everyone gives roughly the same reason – escape.

They might phrase it differently, they might say they want relief from pressure, or they want to get away from the grind of daily life, or they want to get away from a difficult situation, and so on. But it almost always boils down to the need for escape. Surprisingly few people say that they drink just because they like the feeling of getting drunk.

Naturally, heavy drinkers will also want to escape feelings of withdrawal, as we discussed in the chapter on withdrawal cycles. But if it was just a question of dealing with physical withdrawal, then alcohol problems would be very easy to deal with. You would just need to detox for a week, the alcohol would have left your system, the withdrawal would be over, and your problem would be solved.

But of course, it isn't that simple. If it was, then detoxes would always be successful. However, the majority of detoxes are not successful over time. The detoxed person will probably relapse, if not right away, then at a future date. I have met people who have had as many as 10 detoxes in the past and are looking for another. Endless cycles of detox and relapse are achingly painful to go through, and desperately sad to see.

You can take the alcohol out of the body, but if the head is left untreated, relapse is inevitable. This brings me to my Second Law of Recovery from Alcohol Addiction, which states that:

*"Control over alcohol is always dependant on control over emotional responses."*

This is a massive concept. If you have a problem with alcohol and you cannot take this concept on board, you are doomed to a life where alcohol has the upper hand. This is why detoxes often don't work – if you cannot control your emotional responses then relapse at some point is inevitable.

I have heard a thousand stories from drinkers who have relapsed, and 95% of them have been because an emotionally upsetting event had occurred, and they have reached for a drink to cope. Therefore, I believe that the most important skill that a heavy drinker who wants to change can learn is a strategy for dealing with emotionally upsetting events.

How many times have your attempts to control your drinking come crashing down because someone upset you, or something happened to you that you thought was unfair? Perhaps it was unfair, but if you have alcohol problems, whether it was fair or not isn't the issue. What is important is how you respond.

I see so many drinkers going through life being bounced around like the silver ball in a pinball game by their emotional reactions to whatever life throws at them. But it doesn't have to be like that. The key is to get into the habit of responding to events, rather than just reacting in the usual way – by reaching for a drink.

Whenever I hear a story about a relapse – or someone who has been controlling their drinking, but it has suddenly shot back up to previous levels – there is always a reason that comes down to reacting rather than responding.

What I mean by responding is taking an action that is in accordance with your goal of moderation or sobriety rather than simply falling back on the old habits that got you into the problems you face. Let's take a look at the sort of situations that cause problems.

**Unpleasant feelings.**

Firstly, let's talk about unpleasant feelings. Nobody likes to experience anxiety, sadness, loneliness, frustration or anger. But in life, these feelings are bound to crop up, and with great regularity. We wouldn't be human if we didn't experience all of these at some time or other. So, given that these feelings are inevitable and unavoidable, if you reach for a drink every time one of these comes along, your recovery from alcohol addiction is never going to get off the ground.

Rather than trying to numb the feeling with alcohol, think about making a response that will help to address the reason for the feeling. If you are feeling lonely, what can you do to speak to someone who will help you break out of that situation? If you are feeling frustrated, is there something else you can turn your attention to? If you are feeling in a low mood, rather than sit in self-pity, what can you do to put a smile on your face?

You notice I am saying: what can *you* do? Don't sit around waiting for someone else to bring you out of it. You are in the position of power – it's in your hands. You have the control if you can see that you have it.

The solutions to these problems of unpleasant feelings are often very simple. Getting out of your immediate environment is usually a good move. If you are at home, something as simple as going for a walk can change your perspective and break you out of your negative feelings. If you are lonely, you could simply pick up the phone rather than a drink. If you are feeling despondent, you could watch your favourite comedian on YouTube. Don't over-complicate it.

Alternatively, you could watch your mood and let it pass – because it will. This is getting into mindfulness, and we'll be looking at that more in Chapter 15.

**Pleasant feelings.**

The second situation in which people will lift a drink is when they are experiencing pleasant feelings. Feeling good can be a trigger to drink, you want to enhance the experience. As we discussed at the start of this chapter, in the case of "normal" drinkers, this is most often the reason why they drink. But normal drinkers don't overdo it. If you were in that category, you wouldn't be reading this book. Try experiencing and enjoying the good feeling for what it is, and before you reach for that drink, try using the "Play the movie through to the end" technique you learned in Chapter 12.

**Social Pressure.**

The third situation may be social pressure. You may be in a situation where you feel you are the only one who isn't drinking, and you feel the odd one out. But ask yourself, do other people really care? Do they even notice? And if they do, why should you put at risk your recovery, wellbeing and health just to please someone else?

One of my clients, Janine, was planning to go to a wedding. She was going through a period of sobriety, but despite this, she declared:

"I will have to have an alcoholic drink to toast the bride and groom."

I asked Janine: "Why is that?"

Janine looked at me as if I had asked a stupid question. "Because everyone else will be drinking champagne. It will seem odd if I'm just drinking water. I don't want to upset anyone."

I made the following point as we brought the conversation to a close: "Who will be checking what you have in your glass? Who will be offended? Who will even notice when all eyes are on the bride and groom?"

The fact is that other drinkers are only interested in what they are drinking. They don't care what you're drinking. Ask yourself, when you have been on a drinking session, has it bothered you what other people were drinking?

Giving in to social pressure to drink is just people-pleasing. Put yourself first.

**Expectations.**

The fourth situation we will talk about is that of expectations. To explain what I mean by expectations, let's look at a case study. Simon came to me for one-to-one counselling for his drinking. He was a middle-aged man who was living off savings, which were diminishing rapidly as his monthly bar bill was more than $1,000. Financial ruin was looming, but despite this, he couldn't get a grip on his habit, so he wanted my help.

Simon was also very anxious, which is very common among heavy drinkers. The first time we met, he was sweating heavily (again, very common among heavy drinkers), his eyes were bulging, his hands were shaking, and he talked very rapidly in a desire to tell his story and all his problems.

Simon's story was full of examples of how he was the victim of other people's unkindness (at least, that was how he saw it) which gave him a long list of justifications to drink. Simon was drinking to escape negative feelings rather than to enhance positive ones. His list of injustices which he claimed to have endured was exhausting, and I noted that most of them seemed to involve women.

We constructed a plan for him to reduce his drinking and start rebuilding his finances and his life. He was enthusiastic about this, and when we next met he was fired up about how things were going, he had exceeded the targets we had set for week one, his demeanour was that of a man transformed, and everything looked rosy.

Then the following week, Simon almost fell through the door of the consulting room in a state of meltdown as he exclaimed dramatically: "It's all terrible. I've had a terrible week. It's been awful. I haven't slept. And forget about the drinking plan, I've been bang at the drink. I had to have a few beers this morning on the way here. It's all gone wrong."

The shakes and sweating were back, and his demeanour had changed to a look of panic. I thought something truly awful must have occurred. I asked him: "Simon, what on earth's happened?"

Simon sat down heavily with his head in his hands and continued: "It wasn't my fault. I left my ex-wife a message. It was about me going around the house to get a few things I left in the loft when I moved out. It was nothing of hers, just some of my old bits and pieces that I wanted to collect."

I urged Simon to continue.

Simon sighed deeply and carried on: "She rang me back and…. you should have heard her. Swearing at me, screaming, like some animal. She was probably drunk herself; it wasn't just me who was the drinker. She was horrible. Anyway, I had to have a drink and I haven't been able to stop since."

I clarified with Simon: "So this was because your ex-wife rang you?"

He responded with an affirmative: "Yes, I know it sounds a bit weak when you put it like that. But you should have heard her. It was outrageous. She shouldn't be allowed to talk to me like that."

I asked Simon: "When you were together, did she talk to you like that?"

Simon nodded vigorously: "All the time. I told her to go to the doctor. There's something wrong in her head."

"So that's how she used to behave all the time? "I inquired.

With a self-righteous look Simon confirmed: "Yes. You can hardly blame me for getting out of the marriage, can you? I mean, it's just not right."

After a short pause I pointed out: "So, in fact, your ex-wife was behaving as she always does. This is why she is your ex-wife."

The whole reason for Simon's relapse was not his wife's behaviour. She was behaving normally for her. The problem was Simon's expectation that it would be different. He had no reason for this. If he had expected that his wife would be unreasonable, which would have been perfectly logical and in keeping with her normal behaviour, he would not have been upset, because his expectation and her behaviour would have been the same.

Having unrealistic or over-optimistic expectations are just setting yourself up for disappointment.

**Outrage.**

The fifth situation that can push people to give in to cravings is outrage. You don't have to be a problematic drinker to suffer from outrage. It happens to us all, and it can come on quickly and unexpectedly.

Let's take a common enough situation. You are driving along, and someone cuts you up. Suddenly, from being a rational human being, the red mist starts rising and out of nowhere wild thoughts of revenge start flying around your head, the person in the other car becomes the epicentre for all that is evil in your world, you want that driver to rot in the foulest and most disgusting corner of hell.

If you acted on your urges – which probably involve running the other car off the road and thrashing the other driver until they beg forgiveness – who knows where it could lead and what trouble you might bring on yourself. So your rational mind starts to take charge, it tells you to calm down, that the important thing is to get to your destination safely, the other driver was just being stupid and probably didn't mean it – try to forget it. This is what you do. But that feeling of outrage simmers for the rest of the day.

There is nothing like a perceived injustice to bring on outrage and the urge to drink. Everyday life brings many opportunities for that feeling to crop up, such as dealing with bureaucracy, or having to hold on for hours waiting for a call centre to answer you, or the person in front of you at the checkout dithering around. And those are just small things. When life throws a big, real injustice at you, the potential for outrage and alcohol relapse is very real.

This is another case where choosing how to respond, rather than just flying off the handle, will not only keep you away from booze but can potentially save you from an escalating situation that you might live to regret. Try to get yourself away from the situation to give yourself time to calm down enough to think straight. Give yourself time to plan your response, rather than just reacting.

**Blaming others.**

The last situation we will discuss in this chapter is blaming others. It's easy to blame other people for things that go wrong in your life, and therefore your need to drink. It makes you feel better if it was someone else's fault, not your own, as in the following examples:

- It was the barman's fault you got drunk for giving you a drink on the house.

- It was your boss's fault you got drunk. If she hadn't been so hard on you for coming into work late, you wouldn't have got angry and had a drink.

- It was your wife's fault you got drunk because she shouted at you when you crashed the car.

- It's the economy's fault. If it was better, you could afford to have what you want in life and wouldn't drink to drown your sorrows.

- It was God's fault you didn't win the lottery, so you had to have a few whiskies to get over the disappointment.

- It's life's fault you're a drunk. If life wasn't so unfair, you wouldn't need a drink.

It's very easy to pass the blame for your drinking onto other people, or even life, the universe or God. To be able to control your drinking, you need to start by taking responsibility for it. Drinkers don't generally like to take responsibility. Much of their drinking is to avoid responsibility. But if you take responsibility for your actions, you then put yourself in a position of power over your life and your drinking.

## 14. Solution Focused Thinking

When a new client first arrives to see me, they usually float in on a raft of troubles. Although drinking is at the heart of their problems, it's not usually the alcohol itself that has brought them to see me but issues it has created.

High on most people's list are relationships. Many clients have broken relationships in the past, frequently as a result of drinking. They are often separated from their children. Current relationships are suffering too, and the fear of a current relationship breaking down is frequently the motivation for someone coming into treatment.

Mental health, and especially anxiety and depression, are often high on the list of problems. The majority of people I see are on anti-depressants. Anxiety and depression are alcohol's best friends. Wherever alcohol goes, anxiety and depression are usually not far behind. It is one of the great ironies of drinking that most drinkers believe that alcohol cheers them up, when, in reality, continued use of alcohol at high levels virtually guarantees that anxiety and depression will get worse.

Physical health features high in people's concerns, especially as the drinker gets older. They dread going to see the doctor in case they are told they have some horrible alcohol-related condition. I would recommend that any heavy drinker goes and gets honest with their GP and at the very least has a liver function test and general check-up. The physician may then refer you to see a therapist like me for focused treatment.

Money is often a worry, as heavy drinking is not a cheap hobby. It wrecks careers, making money worries worse. And then there are criminal justice worries. Many have had driving bans. Some have long criminal records for alcohol-related offences.

With all this going on in people's minds, it is not surprising that when they arrive to see me, they are very problem-focused. Their worries are swirling around in their minds all the time like some merry-go-round from hell. So they drink even more to numb it out, and the merry-go-round spins even faster.

While being problem-focused is understandable, it has to be changed. Problem-focused thinking is self-defeating. It is often said that you get in life what you think about. This is undoubtedly true when it comes to problems. If you think all the time about problems, you can be sure of what you will get – more problems!

Solution-focused thinking offers the antidote to all this. It's a common-sense way of addressing what is going on in your life, with its roots in proven therapeutic practice. But there is nothing complicated about it. You can easily learn how to do it yourself and apply it not only to sorting out your drinking, but also to any issue in your life.

The origins of solution-focused thinking are in the work of two American social workers, Steve de Shazer and Insoo Kim Berg, and their team at the Milwaukee Brief Family Therapy Center in Wisconsin. Over thousands of hours of analysing therapy sessions, they developed Solution-Focused Brief Therapy. This differs fundamentally from traditional, Freudian therapy, which works on the assumption that it is necessary to analyse the cause of a person's problem before it can be remedied.

I often meet drinkers who are obsessed with finding the root cause of their drinking and feel that they need to do that before they can make any progress with sorting out their drinking. Where this type of approach fails the drinker, however, is that:

Firstly, the drinker might die from alcohol abuse before finding the root cause.

Secondly, if they find the root cause, it might not help them to find a solution.

Thirdly, they discover the root cause, only to realize that the reason they drink now has changed.

Solution-focused thinking does away with all this. As Steve de Shazer said, "Causes of problems may be extremely complex, their solutions do not necessarily need to be."

Let's take an analogy. Imagine you are driving down the road when you drive over a sharp object and get a puncture. If we use the thinking of traditional therapy, we would then have to walk back up the road, find the object and then examine the object to ascertain the root cause of the puncture. But by doing this we are focusing on the problem, not the solution, and we still have done nothing to fix the problem, namely the flat tyre. If we take the solution-focused approach, we simply get out the spare tyre, which is the solution, put it on the car and drive on.

To put solution-focused thinking to work for you, you need to grasp two key concepts, the first of these is 'If it works, do more.'

**If it works, do more.**

In solution-focused thinking, we assume that you, the drinker, might already know the solution to your difficulty, but perhaps without realizing it. It's just a question of uncovering that piece of information. To do this, take a look at what you do now. Are there times when your drinking isn't a problem, even for just a short time? What is going on then? Is what you are doing at that time something you can do more of?

Here's an example from one of my clients. Gloria was a lively 60-year-old in a happy marriage and having a good life. But she had one problem. She told me that for years she had been drinking a bottle of wine every night, often more. She was worried that at her age, this behaviour was catching up with her and that her health was suffering. She was concerned that her friends thought she was an alcoholic and talked about her behind her back. Also, it was causing arguments with her husband. He was an occasional drinker and was worried about Gloria's persistent drinking and her increasingly more outrageous behaviour when she was drunk.

The breakthrough with Gloria came in the following conversation. I began by asking Gloria to tell me about her drinking.

Looking slightly embarrassed, Gloria responded: "I don't know why I do it, really. It's just a compulsion. It gets towards early evening and I just can't think about anything except having a drink."

I confirmed with her: "The thought of drinking obsesses you."

"Exactly. I just need that drink and then, well, I just can't leave the bottle alone once it's open." Gloria sighed, frustrated with her own perceived powerlessness over drink.

I pressed on: "And you say this is what happens every day."

"Yes, every day" Gloria hesitated and added: Well, almost."

"Almost?" I asked." Tell me what you mean by 'almost'."

Gloria continued: "Well, sometimes my friend Moira comes round on a Sunday, and then I don't drink."

I asked: "Why is that? What happens when Moira comes round?"

Gloria informed me: "Oh, we play Scrabble. I don't even think about drinking while I'm playing Scrabble!"

I smiled as I said: "In that case, I suggest you play more Scrabble!"

"Oh, I couldn't play Scrabble every day" Gloria countered and after a brief pause went on: "But maybe a couple of times a week. Moira wouldn't mind."

I nodded: "Great. Now let's talk about what you could do on the other days."

What Gloria had not focused on the problem; we already knew that was drinking. Instead, she had identified a time when the problem went away for a while. She had found an exception, a time when her compulsion to drink went away for a while. From that, we could start constructing a solution. We looked at her playing more Scrabble or taking part in other activities that would engage her brain as Scrabble did. We used the first concept of solution-focused thinking. We found what worked for her, and then found ways she could do more.

Now let's look at a very different case. Gary was a classic black-and-white drinker, by which I mean he either drank to excess, or he didn't drink at all. For Gary, there was no middle-ground. He could no more moderate his drinking than he could fly to the moon. His life was a simple choice between sobriety or self-destruction.

Gary was 55 and his life had been a painful series of periods of abstinence followed by horrible relapses when he would get arrested for fighting. Because of this he had rarely held down a job for long and was unemployed. This made things worse, as alcohol was all he had to think about all day long. When we met, he had just detoxed yet again and was looking for ways to stay sober.

Gary sighed deeply as he said: "My problem is that I can get sober, but then all I think about is drinking. I can go for months without drinking, but then I just find that I have a drink in my hand. I don't know how it happens."

I was keen to express empathy to keep Gary talking. I replied: "It sounds like being sober for you is mental torture."

"That's right, it drives me nuts," Gary responded earnestly.

"But drinking brings you big problems also," I said.

Again, Gary sighed and said with feeling: "I know, I hate drinking as much as I hate being sober. I can't win."

Gary had little chance of seeing a way out of his situation because he was problem-focused. I wanted to find an exception in Gary's history, a time when alcohol wasn't a problem which could be a clue to a solution, so I continued: "Gary. Indulge me for a moment. Cast your mind back. Tell me about a time when you felt content, even if it was just for a short time."

Gary looked thoughtful. After a few moments, he broke the silence. "Well, there was a time about twenty years ago. For about two years, I was all right, really. Life was all right."

I wanted to keep Gary going, so I asked: "Tell me more about those two years. Why were they different from now? What was happening in your life?"

Gary surprised me with his response: "It was all because of the pigs!"

"Pigs! What pigs? "I queried.

Gary carried on, "I was working on a farm looking after the pigs. It was great. I like pigs. I like animals."

"Were you drinking then?" I asked.

Gary shook his head: "No, that was one of my sober periods."

"And you were happy? "I asked. I hoped Gary was starting to join up the dots.

Gary nodded thoughtfully: "Yes, now you mention it, I think I was."

A sudden thought came to me: "There's a farm near here where ex-drinkers like you sometimes go for a while as part of their therapy. They do some voluntary work with the animals, get closer to nature."

Gary listened carefully.

"How would you feel about getting involved in that?" I asked.

He smiled. He liked the idea, so we had the start of a plan for him. Once again, it was the client who had found the solution by looking into the past and finding something that had worked before that could be done again. I had simply assisted in the process.

You can try this yourself. Look back at times when drinking was not a problem. It might be in the distant past. Or it might be that you had a short time recently when you didn't feel the urge to drink. Even if it was only for a couple of hours, it's a start.

Whenever it was, ask yourself:

What was different?

Where were you?

Who were you with?

What were you doing?

Does this show you something you could do now to overcome your excess drinking?

Now we come to the second concept of solution-focused thinking: 'If it doesn't work, do something different'.

**If it doesn't work, do something different.**

When you look at that statement, it seems obvious, doesn't it? If something in your life doesn't work, then you would think it's common sense to do something different. Yet we human beings are constantly repeating actions that don't work for us.

Drinking itself is a prime example. So why exactly is it that so many of us not only drink but drink extraordinary amounts? I think part of the answer lies in the fact that we are talking about an addictive substance and addictions play mind games with you. They make you believe things that only someone with the addiction would believe, things that other people see is nonsense. Like a client who told me, in all sincerity, that drinking 20 pints of cider every day was normal. Even most drinkers wouldn't think that's normal, but he was convinced of it. When we talked further, it emerged that he had been brought up in a pub, where he had seen heavy drinking from a young age and had regarded it as being something good – after all, his father, the pub landlord, made his living from it. But by the time he met me, he had started to get a glimmer of insight that maybe alcohol wasn't working for him anymore, as his health was falling apart. It was time to do something different.

When I meet new clients, they often think there is something wrong with them because they have followed a particular plan and failed. They beat themselves up about it. But as I point out, perhaps it's not you that's failed – it's just that the plan wasn't right for you. It's time to do something different.

For example, I met a woman called Eve, who had been desperately struggling with her drinking for years. She was at her wit's end with it. We had this conversation.

"I'm just a failure. I just can't stop." Eve said in exasperation.

"Tell me, what have you tried? "I asked.

"I go to AA. I've done everything they say." Eve continued: "I have a sponsor. I read the book. I go to lots of meetings. I have a morning routine. But I just can't seem to stay sober for more than a few weeks at a time. I see other women doing well in AA. But I just can't seem to get the hang of it. It must be me. There's something wrong with me."

I asked: "How long has this been going on?"

"Two years" Eve replied: "I've been going to AA for two years."

"What else have you tried? "I asked, waiting for the list to continue.

Eve looked slightly bewildered by the question and responded: "Well, nothing."

For me, this was not an unfamiliar story. I reassured Eve by saying: "I know many people who have done really well in AA. But no one method works for everyone. Even AA doesn't claim that their way works for everyone. After two years, no one could accuse you of not giving it a good try."

Eve looked rather crestfallen as she asked: "Do you think I should stop going? I have friends there."

"I'm not saying stop going" I answered and continued: "Having your sober friends in AA is really helpful. But maybe it would also be helpful to try something different. You could try a course in Cognitive Behavioural Therapy running alongside your AA meetings. And there is a mindfulness course starting soon that I could refer you on to. Would you like some information on those things?"

Eve looked hopeful and agreed to give these other options a try.

To begin with, we see that Eve was problem-focused: she thought she was the problem and was beating herself up about it, which was very unhelpful and just made her feel bad. In the course of this short conversation, she started to focus on solutions, which was far more helpful.

Eve's experience also illustrates that sometimes you benefit from blending more than one approach. In Eve's case, AA was helping in that she had friends who could support her, and she reported that she had had periods of several weeks sober in AA, so she had some success to draw on. By offering additional help and freshening up her approach to staying sober, I hoped to help her get over whatever roadblock she was facing. In fact, she found mindfulness helped and it was complimentary to her AA attendance. (We will be discussing AA more in Chapter 17.)

In your efforts to control or stop your drinking, you have probably tried certain strategies already. Nothing has proved to be totally effective so far, which is why you bought this book. So look at what you are doing to deal with your drinking now. Are there self-defeating behaviours that you are repeating? For example:

Is there one friend you have that always talks you into having a drink when you are don't want to drink? Get a new friend!

Is there a place you visit where you are tempted to drink, like a particular restaurant that has an especially attractive bar? Eat somewhere else!

Is there a particular store you pass on the way home where you always stop off to buy a bottle of wine? Take a different route home!

Can't resist the booze promotions in the supermarket when they are in your face? Shop online!

Now take a look at your regular behaviours. Is there something you are doing that you should just stop right now and do something different? A saying you will often hear in recovery circles is: 'The definition of insanity is repeating the same thing and expecting a different result'. It might be a bit of a cliché, but it's true.

## 15. Stopping those Spinning Wheels

We saw in the last chapter Eve was beating herself up about what she saw as her failure to deal with her drinking. This is not unusual. Repeated battles to tame alcohol lead to drinkers having poor self-esteem. Then, when you finally get to grips with it and achieve a period of sobriety, things can get worse because, as the fog of alcohol lifts, you see in sharper focus all the damage that your career of boozing has done.

As memories of arguments, damage and loss caused by drink come home to haunt you and your self-esteem takes another tumble, then remorse and regret set in. If that wasn't bad enough, as your memory improves, you start getting flashbacks to events that had long been forgotten. It seems like the reasons for putting yourself down just keep piling up higher and higher.

Thoughts of "what if" and "if only" set in.

What if I had done this…

If only I had done that...

The thoughts go round and round like a wheel spinning in your head as you go over past events time and time again. The wheel won't stop spinning because you can never resolve the issues. How can you when they are in the past? You cannot go back in time. You cannot solve what has happened, but your brain keeps trying and that keeps the wheel spinning.

Going over past events you cannot change leads to depression, and depression can lead you back to a drink, putting you in a vicious cycle.

But it's not just past events that can plague you. It's the future, too. You have damaged your prospects. You might find yourself unemployed because of your drinking, or divorced, or in prison. Your mind starts worrying that you have screwed up your future.

Once again "what if" and "if only" come to plague you, but this time it's slightly different:

What if the worst-case scenario happens?

If only a miracle could happen!

You find yourself with another spinning wheel in your head. But this one's focused on the future, on events that may not even happen. Your brain tries hard to solve these puzzles, but as they are in the future, or just in your imagination, your brain can't do it, so this future wheel keeps spinning as well.

Going over imagined future events is where anxiety comes from, and anxiety can also lead to a drink.

So there you are with anxiety and depression, like two wheels spinning in your head. Your normal way of dealing with those issues has always been alcohol, but you have now learnt that while a drink will help tonight, it will only make matters worse in the morning, it is self-defeating. You are caught in a painful place. What can you do?

The answer lies not in the future or the past. It lies in the present.

When we discuss the spinning wheels in my workshops, I draw a couple of big wheels on a flip chart, in the middle of one I write the word "past" and in the other I write "future". Then in between, I write in large letters "NOW" with an arrow pointing to it to indicate that's where we need to focus.

We talk about how – despite all the worries people in the room might have – that right now, at this very moment, we are all okay. We have a nice room, coffee and cookies, each other's company and something interesting to discuss. We talk about how we can create that feeling of wellbeing in the present when we leave the room.

We brainstorm what actions we can take today that will keep us in the present and stop those wheels from spinning. And you, the person reading this book, can do the same thing for yourself. What can you do today to keep yourself in the present?

A good start is simply paying attention to what you are doing and where you are. For instance, when you are walking through your local town along a familiar street, try actively looking around. It's amazing how much detail you see that you've never noticed before, even on a street you've been down a hundred times before. It makes you realize how you are usually so preoccupied and self-absorbed that you miss what's going on around you.

As you walk with a heightened sense of your surroundings, you will notice other people, with hands in pockets and serious faces, looking down at their shoes as they walk – you can bet those people have the wheels spinning in their heads as they walk and are oblivious to what's going on in their present.

A favourite exercise of mine when I am walking through the town is to actively open up my attention to the sounds around me. I am not trying to think about the sounds, I am just trying to be aware of sounds. You realize just how much is happening, the sounds of birds, people talking, traffic, wind in the trees. Paying attention to the present and the world around you gets your mind away from those spinning wheels that cause you to feel anxious or depressed and you feel more balanced and happier.

Think about your activities. What can you be doing that will keep your attention on the present? In the last chapter, we talked about how Gloria found that she didn't even think about drinking when she was playing Scrabble, and how Gary was happy when working with his pigs. They were doing things that kept them centred in the here-and-now.

I had one client, one of the heaviest drinkers I have ever worked with, get over his problems by focusing on learning to play golf. Another found that doing huge jigsaw puzzles worked for him. I knew one woman – who was cross-addicted to alcohol and heroin – who got clean and sober by taking up knitting! The one thing these activities had in common was that it kept people in the present.

Working with other people is a great way of keeping your mind in the present. If you turn your focus to other people, those wheels in your head stop spinning. In drug and alcohol services, we encourage people who have become sober to do a little voluntary mentoring with people new into treatment because it's good for them as well as the people they mentor. Or you can get involved in voluntary work. As well as helping a good cause, you can help yourself by focusing on other people and giving your mind a rest from your own issues.

I know that if I have concerns myself about things that are happening in my own life, one of the best things I can do is go and work with my clients. If my mind is focused on someone I am helping, I cannot think about my own troubles at the same time – it's impossible.

A great way to bring your attention to the here-and-now and stop those wheels spinning is mindfulness. If you've ever thought that mindfulness sounds a bit hippy-ish and woo-woo, consider this: mindfulness is clinically proven to work. Although Mindfulness has been around in the East for thousands of years, the origins of its current popularity in the West owes a lot to the work of Jon Kabat-Zinn, a professor at the University of Massachusetts Medical School, who in the 1980s pioneered Mindfulness-Based Stress Reduction (MBSR) for the treatment of stress, chronic pain and illness. In the UK, it has been recommended by the Health Service since 2005 as a treatment for anxiety that is at least as effective as medication – and you don't get the downside of taking pharmaceuticals.

Mindfulness is a form of meditation that is quite accessible to anyone. It usually begins with turning your attention to your breathing, or sensations in your body, or sounds. It helps you begin observing your thoughts rather than being wrapped up in them. Being detached from your thoughts and looking at them as they come and go through your mind is an experience new to most of us. It gives a detachment and a new level of self-awareness that is really useful to someone struggling with an addiction. Regular practice of mindfulness leads to a generally improved sense of contentment and wellbeing.

Mindfulness has become well-established as a treatment for addictions. Indeed, my clients have found it so helpful that I have written a new book, which I recommend you take a look at when you have finished this book. It's called *"Mindfulness for Alcohol Recovery: Making Peace with Drinking"*. You can find out more and read a free sample on my website – just visit WinsPress.com/books.

## 16. Recruiting your Cheerleaders

Research shows that the majority of people with Alcohol Use Disorder will be able to resolve their problem with little formal help. For instance, earlier in the book we looked at how young people often drink heavily for a few years, but then cut back or stop when major life events happen, such as falling in love, becoming parents, or starting careers. They have found something more meaningful to them than alcohol. This process is known as maturing out. It is simply part of the process of growing up for many people.

Other people, particularly those at the mild end of the Alcohol Use Disorder spectrum, will sort out their issues when they get an alcohol-related wake-up call, like a doctor's diagnosis, relationship problems, or a driving ban. If you are one of those people, you might find that learning a few of the techniques in this book is all the help you need.

## The Importance of Social Support.

Many studies have shown, however, that people who reach out for support are far more likely to succeed in overcoming alcohol issues than people who try to go it alone. At the very least, you need a few cheerleaders: people who will encourage you on the days when it all seems just too difficult. This is why early on in this book I asked you to make public your intention to moderate or stop your alcohol use. This helps you find the cheerleaders in your life.

If you go on to social media and say that, for example, you have decided to stop drinking for three months, this could draw a couple of responses. Some people might say "Rather you than me", "You'll be lucky to last three days" and so on. These people are the doom merchants who have their own alcohol issues. They don't want you to succeed because it makes them feel uncomfortable about their own levels of alcohol use. These people are to be avoided. They will try to poison your mind with negativity. They want to see you fail.

On the other hand, some people will say "Well done", "Good luck" and "What a great idea". These people are golden. You have found your cheerleaders, the people you need to spend your time with. Be honest with your cheerleaders. Share your ups and downs with them. Allow them to cheer you on.

Social media is an increasingly popular source of support. On Facebook, many groups use the platform to cheer each other on. Some are local groups, but most have members from around the globe. You have to be a little careful as these are often not well moderated and there are people out there who are looking to promote their own agendas, which might not be helpful to you.

**Mutual Aid Groups.**

You might consider getting involved with a more structured and established kind of support, known as mutual aid. These are voluntary groups where members can share their experiences and draw support from each other. The colossus of the mutual aid world is Alcoholics Anonymous, or AA, which started in the 1930s and has meetings over most of the world. AA's philosophy is based on a spiritual program called the 12-steps and AA has spawned many other 12-Step groups for other issues. The biggest and best known of these is Narcotics Anonymous, or NA, which covers all drugs, not just alcohol. Then there is Cocaine Anonymous, Gamblers Anonymous, Overeaters Anonymous, Co-dependents Anonymous and numerous others. We will be discussing AA and the 12-Steps in detail in the next chapter of this book.

For many years, AA had the field of mutual aid for drinkers to itself. From the 1970s onwards, however, other rival organisations started to appear. Organisations like Rational Recovery and Life Ring offer a secular alternative to AA's 12-Steps.

Unfortunately, many people in these organisations are so vociferously opposed to AA that a huge ideological bun fight has broken out over the last few decades which I don't think is particularly helpful to people trying to get sober. You don't need to do much research on these organisations on the internet to encounter people with deeply entrenched positions on either side, which is a shame as this draws attention away from the good advice and genuine willingness to help that can be found in all these organisations.

An organisation that has emerged from all these AA alternatives that has also managed to keep itself aloof from the bickering is Smart Recovery. Smart is based around something called Rational Emotive Therapy, a kind of cognitive therapy. Smart is well-run and has established itself outside of its native United States. For example, in the United Kingdom, Smart has become well-established in main-stream treatment and I have facilitated many Smart meetings while working in public health. We will be discussing Smart in detail in Chapter 18.

All these organisations were based on face-to-face group meetings, a model with its roots firmly in the 20th century. The advent of broadband this century, however, brought us a new layer of support. Smart Recovery and AA both have a big online presence, but now we are seeing the emergence of mutual aid that is solely online. A newer player in mutual aid is the Australia-based Hello Sunday Morning which provides support through introducing people with similar goals. On Hello Sunday Morning you sign up with an aim, which could be either sobriety or moderation, and a time frame you want, for example, I want to be sober for 6 months. You will then be invited to link up with others with the same aim.

**Formal Support.**

If you feel you need more formal help, your doctor or local drug and alcohol agency are good places to start. They will be able to assess your needs and refer you to the treatment you require. Usually, what is required is talking therapy in the form of information and alcohol-specific counselling, but if you are physically dependent, they can refer you for medically assisted help.

Depending on your location, help might be state-funded or private sector. If you are using private sector help, ensure that you are dealing with someone registered with the governing body for your country. In the United States, you would look for a substance abuse counsellor who is registered by your state. In the UK, your local health centre and the NHS website will direct you to the alcohol service for your area.

Much of the support available is based around group meetings, either in person or online. Many people are reluctant to attend meetings, which is a shame as research shows that people who isolate are less likely to get over their difficulties, so I would urge you to give meetings a go.

How you react to a meeting is going to depend partly on the skill of the meeting leader, and whether you get on with the other people who attend. But the most important thing is your open-mindedness and willingness to take part.

I get a lot of people who see me for an assessment who panic at the suggestion of attending a meeting. The phrase I hear trotted out is: "It's not for me." Often, the person has never even been to the meeting they say is not for them, so they can't know if that's true. Or maybe they have been to just one or two meetings and been put off by something relatively minor.

This is not just a pity – it's potentially life-threatening. I was talking recently to a member of a mutual aid fellowship who joined years ago with a work colleague, as they were both heavy drinkers. He told me that he had stuck with the group, had been attending meetings for many years, and was now comfortably off and happily retired having enjoyed all the benefits of sobriety. And the colleague? He had decided the meetings were not for him and shortly afterwards had checked into a hotel and killed himself. I can't help wondering if he had persevered with the meetings, there could have been a much happier outcome.

So why do a lot of people struggle with the idea of attending meetings that are designed to help people exactly like them? The most often quoted reason is anxiety. I understand this. Alcohol causes anxiety, so this is not surprising. But it is only by confronting situations that make you anxious that you can overcome anxiety. Ironically, I have often found that it is some of the most anxious people who, when they finally try one of my meetings, enjoy them the most. Also, it's quite funny that it is the people who say "I'll try going to a meeting but I don't want to say anything" who are often the same people who never stop talking once they arrive – you can't shut them up!

I believe, however, that the most common reason for people not wanting to go to meetings is judgmental thinking. People come to a judgment about what the meeting will be like before they even attend. Or they attend but spend the whole time judging the other people at the meeting. We can't help being judgmental. It is a natural human characteristic. Evolution has given us the ability to make snap judgments all the time to protect us from harm. But the judge in your head isn't usually very useful at a recovery meeting.

I recommend that when you attend a meeting, you go with the attitude that you are going to contribute rather than sit in judgment of what you think the meeting can give you. At the very least, you can contribute a spirit of compassion to the meeting even if you say nothing. You might find it much more rewarding as a result. It is a simple shift in perspective that can make a huge difference.

Online meetings make it possible to try out meetings in total anonymity from your living room. Try Googling recovery meetings, AA meetings and Smart Recovery meetings and you will find many to choose from. Keep trying until you find one or two meetings that you like. Indeed, if you are looking for an activity to keep you away from alcohol, doing online meetings every evening could be a great way to fill your time instead of sitting on a barstool. And remember that getting over addiction doesn't have to be all hard work. If you find a meeting that leaves you feeling down, try another meeting; you might find one more to your tastes. A good meeting should leave you feeling inspired.

**Comparing different approaches.**

The common therapies that are used in outpatient facilities like the hospital where I work are called Motivational Enhancement Therapy and Cognitive Behavioural Therapy. These are also used in residential treatment. But in rehabs, Twelve Step therapy is also very common.

All these therapies with fancy-sounding names probably sound baffling.

Which should you sign up for?

A good question – and in fact, it was a question that the United States government spent $27 million trying to answer. It was a study called Project Match, and it was the King Kong of alcohol research studies. There had never been a study of its size before and may never be one again.

How the study worked was that there were three study groups. In each group were drinkers diagnosed with Alcohol Use Disorder. Motivational Enhancement Therapy was used with one group, Cognitive

Behavioural Therapy with another, and Twelve-Step therapy with the third. The reason it was called Project Match was that it wanted to establish if different drinkers should be matched to different programs to improve results. Top-notch therapists were used who were expert in the type of treatment they were delivering.

So which came out on top? Which was the best type of therapy? Well, the answer that came out was:

All of them!

They were all found to be more or less as effective as each other. Interestingly, though, it seems that the most important aspect of the therapy for a lot of the drinkers was not so much the therapy itself as their relationship with the therapist. A logical conclusion of this is that it's really about finding people you are comfortable with, and why a theme of this book is trying to find what is right for you rather than me saying you should do this or that.

Now in the following chapters, let's look at some of these different approaches in more detail.

## 17. AA and the 12-Steps

I meet many people in my work who say AA is wonderful, that it has saved their lives. Equally, I meet many people who just cannot get on with it. AA divides opinion.

One thing that is not in dispute, however, is its size. It is the colossus of alcohol recovery. AA states that it has 117,000 groups, an active membership of more than two million people, and a global reach of 181 countries.

This is fantastic news for AA members, as it means that there is always an AA meeting somewhere near in most parts of the world. Indeed, in large cities, meetings start at breakfast time and can be found all day long. The only other mutual aid organisation that comes anywhere near AA in its amazing coverage of meetings is AA's sister organisation Narcotics Anonymous, which deals with addiction to any drug.

The history of AA started in 1934 with a man called Bill Wilson getting sober in Manhattan. Wilson had spent years drying out and then relapsing. Drinking had wrecked his career on Wall Street and his health, and he was in Towns Hospital for the fourth time. Wilson was under the care of Dr William Silkworth, a man who has a place in AA history for his theory that alcoholism was a combination of mental obsession and physical allergy to alcohol. It was an illness, rather than a personal failing. It was while under Dr Silkworth's care that Wilson received a treatment called the Belladonna cure, a concoction of plants including Belladonna that causes hallucinations.

It was at this time that Wilson had what he called a spiritual awakening. It was a dramatic, white light event. He says in AA's main text that he experienced "such a peace and serenity as I had ever known."

It would be easy to be cynical about the idea of Wilson having some sort of psychological upheaval under the influence of a hallucinogenic drug. But whatever happened, there is no doubt that Wilson had a dramatic shift in perspective and didn't drink again until he died in 1971. What followed from that day in 1934 was going to help millions of people. Time Magazine posthumously named Wilson as one of the 100 most influential people of the 20th Century.

In 1935 Wilson turned his attention to helping other hospitalised drinkers. History tells us that he didn't succeed in getting anyone sober, but he discovered that this was a great way of keeping himself sober. This makes a huge amount of sense. I have recommended in this book working with other people as a way of helping yourself. If you are thinking about other people, it is impossible to be thinking about yourself at the same time, which can be very helpful in recovering from alcohol addiction. The concept of "doing service" has become enshrined in AA, with members given jobs to help their group to function: it could be making the coffee, or maybe looking after the group's accounts. The important thing is that it gives the individual a sense of purpose and turns their attention to helping others.

A few months into his sobriety, Wilson found himself away from home on a business trip and was tempted to drink. He set out to find another alcoholic he could work with, to help take away his own urge to drink. This led him to meet Dr Robert Smith, an extreme drinker, just as Wilson had once been. Their relationship blossomed, Smith got sober, and Bill and Bob became the founding fathers of a fellowship that at that time had no name.

Their fellowship started to grow as new members joined, originally meeting at Wilson's house. Eventually, the membership reached about 100. Wilson and the others set about writing a book about their experiences which was published in 1939. This book, which AA members usually call the Big Book, was officially called "Alcoholics Anonymous" and the fellowship found its name. It also found a lot of publicity when in 1941 the Saturday Evening Post ran an article about Alcoholics Anonymous, and AA took off.

AA meetings vary in terms of their format, but one thing common to all meetings is the concept of "sharing", which simply means having your say. Debating isn't allowed. You can have your turn to speak but then are expected to be quiet to give someone else a chance. AA is a kind of therapy with a story-telling tradition. Members share what is often called their "experience, strength and hope". This frequently involves going into quite graphic detail about their drinking past, which are often called war stories. Some people find it helpful to hear other people's war stories, while others say that they make AA meetings seem negative. You need to make your own decision on this.

Anyone can join AA. As they say in AA, "the only requirement for membership is a desire to stop drinking". And they do mean stop. AA is an abstinence program. If you went there talking about moderation, you could expect a frosty reception. It doesn't cost you anything to join. They usually take a collection to cover the cost of running the meeting, like hiring the room and providing coffee and biscuits for physical meetings or website costs for online support.

Central to AA's way of working is that all meetings are self-funding and autonomous. Any two members getting together can start an AA meeting. As long as they adhere to AA traditions, they don't need to make any formal application to AA.

Although you don't make any sort of financial commitment when you join AA, if you become a regular, you are expected to help run your local group. For long-standing members with stable sobriety, it could mean running the meeting, or even organising for AA on a regional or national level.

I find AA's way of self-funding and autonomy on a local basis refreshing in its independence. One of AA's traditions is "declining outside contributions". You won't see a "donate" button on the AA web site.

AA is very much an organisation run by its members for its members. The officers of AA are all elected by their peers and, except for a few administration posts, are unpaid. Anonymity, as the name Alcoholics Anonymous suggests, is a core tradition. Your attendance at meetings is not recorded and nobody asks for your second name. Even Bill Wilson was known as Bill W within the fellowship during his lifetime.

Whilst this helps to ensure your privacy, it means that there is no vetting of people in AA, so it's a good idea not to divulge personal information. AA literature talks about disclosing your story in a general way, which would seem good advice if you don't know everyone in the meeting. And it's also worth bearing in mind when you are looking for help from members of the group that AA is a fellowship of peers. Therefore, the people are there because they have a similar problem to you, which doesn't qualify them as therapists. Advice from other members may be well-intentioned, but there is no quality control on people's opinions. Fortunately, AA is backed by much literature and advice that members can refer to.

When you go to AA, you will hear standard advice like "don't pick up the first drink", or "one day at a time" or "keep coming back to meetings". It's a simple message that has kept many people sober for years. But AA goes much deeper than that. Central to AA's philosophy is the 12 Steps. This is a program of recovery that has its roots in an evangelical organisation which pre-dates AA called the Oxford Group, of which Bill Wilson had been a member.

This is where a lot of resistance to AA comes in, because there is no getting away from the fact that in the Big Book and the 12 Steps there is a lot of talk about God, which puts many people off. But I should say that in AA the concept of God is not a religious one. AA says that it is "a God of your understanding", so it is something that makes sense to you. It is what AA calls a power greater than you or a higher power. It can be what you want. It can be nature or the universe. It can be a higher form of you. AA likes to say that it is a spiritual program, not a religious one.

To many people, the concept of having a higher power and a spiritual program sounds like so much hocus pocus and they reject AA outright because of that, cutting themselves off from the biggest support group on the planet for problematic drinkers. I think there is a lot of misunderstanding because of the terminology used, and that the language of AA goes back to the 1930s.

How I try to explain AA to drinkers who have never attended is that AA encourages you to put your faith in a higher power and live one day at a time. This higher power can be could be your plan for recovery from your addiction. If I suggested to you putting your faith in your plan and living one day at a time, you would probably think that sounds sensible and not like hocus pocus at all.

Looking at this from a scientific point of view, this is likely to result in less stress and anxiety and better outcomes. If you are focusing your attention on the day in hand rather than projecting ahead, you are likely to make a better job of whatever you are doing, hence the likelihood of a better result.

This is something that people pay money to achieve through Cognitive Behavioural Therapy, Mindfulness, or Life Coaching but is available from AA for free. And having a healthy spiritual attitude to life is an indicator of good mental health.

However, it isn't necessary to follow the spiritual program to attend AA, so if you are unsure, I would not let it put you off. There are a lot of people out there living their lives by the 12-Steps and are very grateful for it. But many other members don't follow the 12-Step program. As they say in AA, you can take what you need and leave the rest.

I think the antiquated language of the Big Book is a big problem for AA in this century. But the members seem to like its old-fashioned language. Change happens very slowly in AA. Even in the very early days when AA was so small that the members could all meet at Bill Wilson's house, Wilson discovered the members very reluctant to change. Wilson himself was a radical and he found conservatism in the organization frustrating.

The upshot of this is that the language of AA's core text, written in the 1930s, becomes more difficult to understand for new members with every year that passes. The Big Book also gets a lot of criticism – including from AA members – for being sexist. I doubt it was seen that way when it was written, but it is now. However, as so many members treat the Big Book more like a sacred text than a self-help book, it is unlikely to change any time soon.

If you have never been to AA and want to stop drinking, it is worth your time going to see what it's all about. All you need to do is Google AA meetings in your area and turn up with an open mind – as simple as that. Many local groups run online meetings, which give an easy way to explore AA. As long as you have a desire to stop drinking, you will be welcome.

If you are one of the people who can get on with AA, you will have found yourself a huge resource, somewhere you can make like-minded sober friends, and find unparalleled worldwide support.

But AA is not the only option available. In the next chapter, we will investigate a science-based alternative: Smart Recovery.

# 18. Smart Recovery and the 4-Point Program

SMART Recovery® has its roots in the AA alternatives that started towards the end of the last century and seems to be the most successful of the bunch. Smart stands for Self-Management and Recovery Training. The Smart Program was put together by a collaboration of professionals and people in recovery and launched in 1994. It is very practical.

Smart is not so much one original philosophy as a collection of techniques that have been assembled to make one program. At its heart is something called Rational Emotive Behaviour Therapy, or REBT, which was created by a psychiatrist called Albert Ellis. REBT focuses on our thinking habits and rooting out the kind of faulty thinking that often leads to drinking.

Smart has built around REBT many recovery support and relapse prevention strategies, which it calls the Smart tools. The whole program, which Smart likes to call science-based, is flexible in that as new breakthroughs in recovery are made, they can be added to Smart. For example, mindfulness has started to make an appearance in Smart. The whole program can be found in the Smart Recovery Handbook, which is updated on a regular basis, as is the website smartrecovery.org, which is packed with resources.

Smart's strap-line is "The Power of Choice". In Smart's philosophy, if you have chosen to maintain an addictive life, you can choose to stop it. There is much talk of self-empowerment. The Smart program has the following 4-point structure:

1. Building and Maintaining Motivation.

2. Coping with Urges.

3. Managing Thoughts, Feelings, and Behaviours.

4. Living a Balanced Life.

Smart is not specific to alcohol, it covers any drug and also any addictive behaviour, so it could be applied to anything from heroin to gambling to smartphone addiction. But as alcohol is the giant of the addiction world, there is plenty in Smart for the drinker. It is abstinence-based, but it does leave the door open for people who are not committed to abstinence to come in and take a look.

A Smart meeting is led by a facilitator, whose job it is to ensure the smooth running of the meeting and keep it relevant to Smart's principals. The facilitator is Smart-trained. Smart runs a thirty-hour online training course from Ohio to skill up facilitators. As I have done this course myself, I can confirm that it's a thorough, well-constructed course, and this means that there is consistency and quality-control between Smart meetings wherever you attend one.

If the Smart meeting is based in a treatment facility, such as the out-patient location I work in, the facilitator may be a recovery professional like myself. However, ideally, Smart meetings will be peer-led, meaning that the facilitator will probably be someone who entered Smart initially as a service-user. In this way, Smart can grow organically.

Smart meetings follow a standard format. This begins with a check-in, at which participants can share their ups and downs, usually focusing on recent events. Unlike the 12-Step tradition, in Smart the telling of war stories is discouraged. Smart also discourages the use of labels like alcoholic or addict. At the end of the check-in, the facilitator will draw up an agenda for discussion, based on key points that participants have talked about in the check-in, and the meeting will be open for discussion.

So for example, let's say that boredom as a trigger to drink had come up as an issue for people in the check-in, the facilitator might lead a group brainstorm (a common Smart technique) to come up with solutions to this, perhaps ending up with a flip chart full of helpful ideas. The meeting would then move on to the next agenda item. It is part of the facilitator's role to keep the discussion flowing and to relate issues raised by the participants to tools in the Smart program. The meeting finishes with a checkout, at which participants can reflect, for example, on what they have learned from the meeting or plans for the week ahead. A hat might be passed for donations to help finance the meeting.

As part of my work for government-commissioned services in England, I have been facilitating Smart Recovery meetings for four years. During this time I have seen a lot of drinkers and users of other drugs pass through the meetings. I have found that Smart has been well-received. The one area that people sometimes struggle with is that Smart can use a lot of rather academic language and it loves its acronyms (Smart itself being an acronym) which people can find confusing. But that aside, people generally seem to take well to Smart.

I was once asked to facilitate a Smart meeting I had never previously attended. As I didn't know the people in the room, I wanted to get an idea for how much they knew about the Smart Program, so I asked what they understood about the Smart program.

I got an immediate response from one person: "Learning how to handle PIGs and DIBs." I thought this was great, as it does sum up a lot about what Smart teaches.

A PIG is a *Problem of Immediate Gratification.* A person with an addiction is someone who is used to immediate gratification – when the urge to drink comes on, you want to get that drink right away. If you can't get that drink, it starts to be difficult to think of anything else, it becomes a craving. But every time you give in to that craving, the problem gets worse, your PIG gets bigger, then before you know it, your life is all about feeding your huge PIG. In Smart, you work on how to put control back in your own hands and take it away from the PIG.

DIB is short for *Disputing Irrational Beliefs.* An irrational belief is one of those it-was-a-good-idea-at-the-time thoughts that can get you into trouble if you act on them. When the idea pops into your head, it might sound reasonable. But if the thought came from your addiction, watch out! So how do you spot an irrational belief and what do you do about it?

An irrational belief is:

- Unrealistic, there is no evidence to support it,
- When you look at it carefully, it doesn't make sense,
- It's harmful to you and will sabotage your goals.

The way to deal with an irrational belief is to turn it into a question, then give an answer, like this:

Irrational belief: "I'll die if I don't get a drink." Now turn this into a question such as: "Will I really die if I don't have a drink?" Your answer could be: "No, I won't die – I'll just feel uncomfortable for a while. In fact, I'm more likely to die if I do have a drink."

Here's another example of an irrational belief: "I haven't had a drink for a week, so I'll be okay to go and see the guys at the bar. I'll just have an orange juice." Turn this into the following question: "Will I really just have orange juice?" Your answer might sound like this: "Who am I trying to kid? I've never drunk orange juice with those guys ever! This is just my addiction trying to fool me into picking up a drink."

A further example of an irrational belief could be: "I drive better if I've had a drink because I feel more relaxed." Turn this into the following question: "Do I really drive better if I've had a drink?" The following might be your answer: "No, I just feel like I do. The reality is that my reactions are poorer like everyone else. I could lose my licence or worse – I could kill someone."

We will consider two further examples to illustrate how we can shed some light on irrational beliefs by turning them into questions: The irrational belief might be: "My life is such a mess, I deserve a drink." You could turn it into this question: "Do I really deserve a drink because my life is a mess?" The answer you might get is: "No, my life is a mess because of my drinking. Having more to drink is likely to make it worse."

And finally you might relate to this irrational belief: "I need a drink because I'm bored." Turn this into the question: "Will a drink really help with boredom?" Your answer could be: "No, I'll just end up bored and drunk. The cure for boredom is finding something to do."

I hope you get the idea now of how to dispute irrational beliefs. If you like, you could have some fun with DIBs and think up some of your own. Think back to the last time you had an unplanned drink that you regretted. Was there an irrational belief to blame? Can you remember what it was? If it happened again, how would you dispute it?

The examples I have given only relate to drinking, since that is what this book is about. But if you practice disputing irrational beliefs, you can turn it into a skill that can benefit every part of your life.

The problem you might have with Smart is in getting to a face-to-face meeting. It simply doesn't have the global reach in that respect of AA and the other larger 12-Step organizations, especially outside the USA. If you can't get to a physical meeting, try an online meeting. Smart is well geared up for this, and as with the physical meetings, the facilitators of the online versions are Smart-trained.

As mentioned earlier, Smart owes a lot to the work of the psychiatrist Albert Ellis, and his ideas are also fundamental to Cognitive Behavioural Therapy. So let's look at that next.

# 19. Cognitive Behavioural Therapy (CBT)

Cognitive Behavioural Therapy, usually called CBT, is a talking therapy that is frequently used to treat addictions as well as conditions like anxiety, phobias, depression, and PTSD. I am including it in this book because its use in addiction therapy is so widespread and, although you are better seeing a professional CBT counsellor to get best results, you can gain a lot from grasping a few basic CBT concepts right now.

CBT treats emotional disturbances. This is important from the point of view of the drinker as research shows that most problematic drinkers overuse alcohol as a way of dealing with emotional upsets. True, you can drink because of good news, but mostly it is to shut out the bad.

A basic belief in CBT is that you feel how you think. Those emotional disturbances come from your thoughts and opinions. To illustrate this, let's take the example of a big sporting event like a football final. At the end of the game, the followers of the winning side will be in a euphoric emotional state, cheering and clapping, whereas the followers of the losing side will be in a negative emotional state, frowning and with their shoulders slumped.

But why should this be? After all, they have both seen the same game. It is simply because the fans of the winners will have the thought that the result was good and will feel good, whereas the fans of the losers will believe the result to be bad and will feel that way. Therefore, what you believe about something does indeed dramatically affect your emotional state.

CBT is very practical and indeed a lot of CBT seems like common sense when it is pointed out to you. With a little knowledge, you can start to become your own therapist simply by being able to spot common traps that our thinking often falls into, causing emotional distress. So let's look at some common forms of unhelpful thinking. These are situations that can affect anyone, not just drinkers. But if drinking is a problem for you, these mind traps can easily bring on a relapse or a bout of heavy drinking that makes matters much worse. Listen to the following examples of mind traps and try to identify instances where you might have been caught out in the past.

**Mind Trap 1: Black and White Thinking.** When you engage in black and white thinking, you believe that everything depends on one thing. "I'll never be happy until I get a new house." Or "I can't relax until all my debts are paid." This kind of thinking puts all your eggs in one basket and sets you up for serious disappointment, which can lead to heavy drinking. It is never the case that everything depends on one thing.

**Mind Trap 2: Ignoring the Positives.** When you ignore the positives, you focus on negative things that happen and filter out the good stuff, such as thinking, "Nothing ever goes my way." When you ignore the positives that happen in your life, you build in your mind the idea that you are a victim. But positive things happen to everyone, so this is untrue.

**Mind Trap 3: Negative Self-Labelling.** Putting a label on yourself is unhelpful. For example, if you label yourself an alcoholic or an addict, this can lead to self-sabotaging thinking, such as, "I'm an alcoholic and there's nothing I can do about it."

**Mind Trap 4: Catastrophizing.** When we catastrophize, we imagine the worst-case scenario all the time and that catastrophe is sure to happen. For example, you might think that "If I don't get that new job, I won't be able to pay the bills and my wife will leave me." In reality, although the worst can sometimes happen, it usually doesn't.

**Mind Trap 5: Mind Reading.** This is the mistaken belief that you know what other people are thinking. For example, "I know they all hate me at that meeting. You can see it by the looks on their faces." Sometimes you might guess right, but mostly you will be wrong. You can cause yourself a lot of emotional distress because you believe people are thinking something that they are not.

**Mind Trap 6: Self-Pity.** When we engage in self-pity, we waste our time lamenting how unfair life is, such as "It isn't fair the way they treat me." Or "It shouldn't be like that." Self-pity is caused by the irrational belief that life should be how you want it to be, which leads to disappointment. This thinking is always self-defeating and one of the main causes of relapse.

**Mind Trap 7: Approval Seeking.** This means basing your value as a person on what other people think. You are always seeking praise and feel crushed when you don't get it. It's pleasant if other people think well of you, but if your self-esteem relies on the good opinions of other people, you are asking for trouble.

**Mind Trap 8: Ignoring the Present.** When we ignore the present, we are constantly prioritizing the future over our current needs. For instance, "I can't think about taking a break now, because I need to get things done for next week." You end up feeling overwhelmed, which is a major trigger for drinking.

**Mind Trap 9: Dwelling on Past Pain.** When we focus on upsetting past events, we are staying in a painful place rather than living our life as it is today. For instance, "I'll never be happy until I work out where I went wrong." This opens the trap door to the downward spiral of depression and drinking.

**Mind Trap 10: Fortune Telling.** This means believing that you can see into the future, such as "There's no point in trying to stop drinking. I know I'll fail." Unless you are genuinely clairvoyant, I suggest putting away the crystal ball. Fortune telling just leads to self-defeating thinking.

**Mind Trap 11: Blame Shifting.** This means not taking responsibility for your actions. When something goes wrong, it's always someone else's fault, such as "If she hadn't upset me, I wouldn't have relapsed." If you avoid taking responsibility for your behaviour, you will always be vulnerable to relapse.

**Mind Trap 12: Super-Optimism.** This is assuming that something will be okay even though the evidence is to the contrary. A common example with alcohol is thinking "I'll just have one drink, then stop" when that has never happened before.

A method that is used in CBT to combat thinking errors is called the ABCs, which Albert Ellis developed back in the 1950s. Ellis was looking for a way of working with his clients that would produce much quicker results than traditional therapy. This technique is a core skill in both CBT and Smart Recovery. It works like this:

**A** stands for Activating Event: This is an actual external event which happens in real life that sets off an emotional response. It could also be a thought or fear about an imagined future event that sets off a reaction.

Or it could be an internal event in your head, like a memory or an idea.

**B** stands for your Belief about the Activating Event. So for example, if A – the Activating Event was a strong craving for alcohol, your B might be the Belief that you must have a drink to get rid of the craving.

**C** stands for the Consequences of A and B – The Activating Event and the Belief: So following on from the given example, a strong craving for alcohol is the Activating Event and your Belief is that you must have a drink to get rid of the craving then the Consequence will be having a drink.

So how does this ABC model help?

If you can recognize the Activating Event and the Belief, you can question the Belief. You examine the evidence as to whether or not it is true. In the above example, if you challenged the evidence of the Belief that you must have a drink to get rid of the craving, you might then conclude that, in fact, it isn't true and you do not need to take a drink. If you just did something to distract yourself for a few minutes, then the craving would fade away. You would then end up with a different Consequence, which would be that you didn't have a drink.

When I am doing the ABCs with a group, I like to develop what I call cascading ABCs. This is where one ABC leads on to another. It can take you a long way in terms of consequences. Here is an example.

The Activating Event is that the phone rings as you are relaxing at home. It's your ex who wants to change the access arrangements to see the kids at the weekend.

Your Belief is that you think this is out of line. You have something arranged for the weekend.

The Consequence of this Activating Event and Belief is that you have a fight on the phone.

You could have examined the evidence for your Belief, in which you think your ex is being unreasonable. Was your ex being out of line, or was there actually a good reason? Could there have been a compromise that could have suited you both and the kids? However, you flew off the handle and next, the Consequence is that you have a fight and so the fight becomes the next Activating Event, which leads onto the next Belief in which you think:

"This is outrageous how dare he speak to me like that! I need a drink!". This Belief then follows on to the next Consequence in which you go to the store and buy a bottle of wine. You drink the wine and want more – this is the next Activating Event. This leads to the Belief that you can drive to the store for another one. It's not far. You'll be okay, you think. This false Belief that you are safe to drive goes unchallenged by you and this leads to the next Consequence, which is a car crash and legal trouble.

You could have looked at the evidence for your Belief, which was that you are not safe to drive when you have drunk a bottle of wine – it's just the booze talking. This moment of reflection on your Belief might have been enough to halt the whole cascade of Activating Events, Beliefs and the unfortunate Consequences.

You can see how the ABCs cascade one into another. In the scenario just discussed, this could continue to cascade until you lose your job or end up with a prison sentence, and this could all have been avoided if you had just questioned your Belief that your ex was being unreasonable on the phone, by questioning the evidence.

This gives you an overview of some of the basics of Cognitive Behavioural Therapy. There is much more to CBT that is beyond the scope of this book, which you can explore with a CBT counsellor. But even if you can just master what you have read in this chapter, you can make big strides in controlling your drinking and in your life generally.

## 20. Relapse Prevention

We have covered a lot of ground in this book. We have looked at how society and advertising condition our thinking about alcohol; we have exploded common alcohol myths; we have discussed Alcohol Use Disorder, and have investigated different treatment methods and useful drugs; we have explored the pros and cons of moderation and sobriety, detox and reduction, withdrawal cycles and how time can perform wonders with your body and mind if you give it a chance; we have gone into the head game of overcoming alcohol, using many techniques like solution focused thinking and mindfulness; we have compared AA, Smart Recovery, and Cognitive Behavioural Therapy-based treatment.

In the introduction to this book, we talked about how alcohol can seem like a huge overpowering dark force that always gets the upper hand, but how demystifying alcohol takes away its power. I hope that having read this book, you find that alcohol is demystified for you now and you feel equipped to take the power back into your own hands. I hope that you have a plan and are starting to make progress.

But what's next?

Alcohol Use Disorder is by its very nature a relapsing condition and inevitably most people don't beat it at the first attempt. There can be many slips along the way. This is normal. If you have a slip, this is not something to beat yourself up about. Apply solution focused thinking. Look at what happened. What worked, if only for a while, that you can do more of? What didn't work and what can you do differently?

But how can you avoid the pain of a full-blown relapse? Opinions differ on what exactly constitutes a relapse, but I would define it as follows: A relapse is where you return to your original behaviour for several days. What exactly that original behaviour was, only you know.

If you have been abstinent from alcohol, then relapse is obvious: you are drinking alcohol again. The remedy is to put the alcohol down right away. Don't start thinking "Oh, I'll just have a few today and start again tomorrow" or "It'll be okay just for the weekend". The more you drink the harder it will be to stop again. The voice in your head that is telling you that it's okay to have a few is the voice of your addiction, and your addiction wants to destroy you.

If you have gone down the route of moderation, a relapse can be trickier to see starting. It might just be one extra drink above your self-imposed drinking limit.

In this case, the voice of your addiction can sound very soothing and beguiling "Oh, it was only an extra one, you're doing well, and it won't hurt". But it will hurt. Before you know it, you will be back to drinking at your problematic level, while your addiction is telling you lies like "It's okay, you can cut back again tomorrow".

In the early days of your recovery plan, a relapse can happen very quickly. It might take a few attempts to get your plan off the ground. But as your plan starts to get going and you have days and then weeks of achievement under your belt, it's easy to become a little over-confident.

Relapse can be a subtle foe. It doesn't always happen suddenly. Indeed, the longer you get into your plan, the more likely it is that relapse takes its time. If you can spot the early signs, you can nip it in the bud before it takes hold. Here are warning signs to look out for:

**Warning sign 1.** You start finding reasons not to do the things that have been working for you. For instance, if you have been going to lots of recovery meetings and you suddenly start to cut back. Or maybe you have been seeing a counsellor and you start thinking you are too busy to see her anymore. Or you have been going to yoga or meditation groups, and you stop. Whatever it is, have a serious talk with yourself, ask yourself if there is really a good reason for this behaviour change, or are you starting to backslide?

**Warning sign 2.** You start seeing old drinking friends or visit places where you used to drink. You might tell yourself that you can do this now, you have done well, and you are strong. But is this really you that's talking, or is it the voice of your addiction? You might be able to see those people or go to those places at some date in the distant future, but if you are just weeks into your plan, it is much too dangerous. Ask yourself if it is really a desire to drink that is drawing you closer. Are you courting relapse because, deep inside, you want to find an excuse to drink?

**Warning sign 3.** You think about the good times you had drinking and romanticising your past. You forget all the terrible things that alcohol brought into your life. This leads you to feeling hard done by. It makes you think that life is unfair. You should be able to enjoy yourself. Self-pity starts to take hold, and before you know it, the voice of your addiction is putting up powerful arguments for drinking. It starts telling you that you are better with a drink, you are wittier, you have more fun, and other enticing lies. If this happens, take a piece of paper, write down all the horrors that alcohol caused you on one side. On the other side, write down all the benefits that your new life is bringing you. Then compare the two.

**Warning sign 4.** You start thinking that perhaps things weren't as bad as they seemed. You think you can cut corners. You wonder if the reasons why you took action on your drinking were exaggerated. You wonder if all those dire health warnings you read about alcohol are all so much hot air. You begin to think that you don't need to keep following your plan. You're okay now.

You deserve a break. One day off the plan won't hurt. In short, you start to think that all you have learnt doesn't apply to you.

This leads us to my Third Law of Recovery from Alcohol Addiction:

**"You are not an exception."**

The idea that everything you have heard doesn't apply to you has launched a billion relapses. Ask yourself, what evidence is there that I am different? Why should I be able to get away with drinking now in a way I couldn't in the past? Where's the proof?

Finally in this chapter, I must cover a different reason for relapse: Post-Acute Withdrawal Syndrome. In my professional experience, this is very common, yet surprisingly few of the clients I talk to have ever heard of it even though they might have experienced it. Indeed, many of my fellow recovery professionals know little about it. But if you understand what it is, you can save yourself a relapse and much pain.

In the early stages of giving up any addictive substance, you expect to suffer from withdrawal. It's no surprise. This is called the acute stage, when the substance is still in your body, but the levels are dropping. In the case of alcohol, it takes about 10 days for the body to be completely rid of the drug.

However, you will find that you still feel like you are in withdrawal from time to time afterwards. These feelings can come in waves. This can be confusing because you know that alcohol can't be in your body any longer.

What is happening is that your brain chemistry is readjusting after a long period of alcohol abuse. It is normal, but it feels like something is going wrong. What's more, Post-Acute Withdrawal Syndrome can occur for anything up to two years after you stop drinking. Most people don't know that. A client of mine, Pamela, explained her experience with Post-Acute Withdrawal Syndrome like this:

*"Getting into recovery from alcohol was much easier than I had expected. The first couple of weeks were difficult – I often felt as though I didn't know what to do with myself. But that soon passed. I had heard ex-drinkers say that when you stop drinking a lot of people get what is called a 'pink cloud' period, when everything seems lovely, and that is what happened to me.*

*The world without alcohol just seemed marvellous. I absolutely loved the feeling of being clean and clear-headed. Everything seemed so colourful. My senses seemed to have been heightened.*

*I went to recovery meetings all the time, five or six a week. It didn't matter which ones. I went to AA, NA, Smart, and meetings at the local drug project. I loved hearing other people's stories. Some were real eye-*

*openers, especially people who had been cross-addicted. But it didn't matter how gritty the stories were, and even if they were very different from me, I got a lot from them. In fact, if I couldn't go to a meeting for a few days, I really missed them. They were a vital part of my recovery.*

*During all this time, I had days when I would feel the urge to drink, lots of them. But I just kept myself busy, which helped a lot. I didn't give myself time to think about it. Something that had been drummed into me at meetings was not to allow self-pity a chance to take over my head, and that was good advice. The urges would always pass pretty quickly.*

*It all went well and before I knew it, I was a year sober. I was still keeping busy. I was helping out at some of the groups I attended. I had made lots of sober friends. Life was good.*

*Then it happened. Completely out of the blue one morning I woke up with a raging craving to drink, as bad as anything I could remember in my first few days after quitting. But this was after about 16 months of sobriety.*

*I was devastated. I started to panic. My thoughts were that it had all been a waste of time. All the meetings I had been to, all the good things I had done was all for nothing. Alcohol had come back to claim me. And it didn't go away. I was in tears. I felt beaten; alcohol had got me. It all seemed so unfair.*

*It would have been easy to pick up a drink that day. I just felt like giving up the battle with alcohol. But I didn't. Instead, I rang up a therapist who had given me some counselling in my early days. Luckily, he was available. When he heard what was happening, he told me to come and see him that afternoon.*

*When I saw him, the cravings were still raging. I told him the full story. He told me not to panic. He said it sounded like Post-Acute Withdrawal Syndrome. I said I had never heard of it. He explained that it was just my mind settling. That it would pass. I was just to stick to my normal routine. He was right. It took a week, but it did pass. Thankfully, it never returned."*

Here's how to manage Post-Acute Withdrawal Syndrome:

Firstly, expect that it could happen to you. That way you won't be in a panic as Pamela was.

Secondly, if it does happen, don't think that something has gone wrong. Although it feels bad, it's a sign that something is going right. It is your brain recalibrating and returning to normal.

Lastly, stick to your routine and trust in the things that have kept you sober up until that point. It will pass.

You are nearing the end of your journey through this book. In the next chapter, we will look at your future.

## 21. Now the Nightmare is Over, What Do You Want the Dream to Be?

Being a heavy drinker takes a lot of time, money and effort. Leaving alcohol behind creates time and opportunity in your life. It's now up to you to decide how you want to enjoy that time.

On one level, it's important to keep up the practices that have helped you. Don't drop any practices that have worked for you unless you are sure they really have passed being useful. For example, if you went to lots of recovery meetings, cut back on them by all means if you think you don't need to attend so many, but don't just stop. That could trigger a relapse.

On another level, however, it's important to start getting on with your life. Recovery from alcohol is often described as being a bridge to normal living. It is not normal living in itself. I have met many people who seem to have got stuck in a recovery bubble and, while they might not be drinking any more, you wouldn't really describe them as being sober. It's time to move your focus away from alcohol altogether. Try this exercise:

Take a notebook and find somewhere you won't be disturbed. Do a little brainstorming just with yourself. Ask yourself, now the nightmare is over, what do you want the dream to be?

Keep writing until you have a long list and have exhausted your mind of all the things you might want to do. Now go through your list. Put a circle round the ones that appeal to you the most.

Next, draw up a shortlist. Then number them in order of preference. Keep working on your list until one thing emerges as the number one thing you want to do with your sober life, something that will inspire you and make it all worthwhile.

You are looking into your future at the glittering prize that awaits you at the end of your sober adventure.

Go and get it now.

Congratulations, you have now reached the end of Alcohol and You. But this is not the end of support from me. On my website, I regularly post articles and downloadable audios that supplement the information you have discovered in this book. This is all free. Simply go to WinsPress.com and look under the 'Free Stuff' tab.

Neither is it the end of this book, as I have included bonus chapters for you to, so keep reading.

I wish you well on your journey.

# My Three Laws of Recovery from Alcohol Addiction.

1. Misery increases in direct proportion to the amount of alcohol taken.

2. Control over alcohol is always dependent on control over emotional responses.

3. You are not an exception.

# Bonus Chapters

That brings us to the end of "How to Control and Stop Drinking" part of *Alcohol and You*, but not the end of this book.

After writing the book you have read so far, I wrote another short book to supplement the information in *Alcohol and You*. This was called: *Reversing Alcoholism: Real Recovery from Alcohol Addiction*. Although the subject was again problem drinking, this was a very different book. It is not a "how to" book. It looks at what actually happens out there to people who decide to take on their alcohol difficulties.

As a special thank-you to you for buying *Alcohol and You*, I am including on the following pages an abridged version of *Reversing Alcoholism* for you to learn from and, I hope, also enjoy.

# Reversing Alcoholism

Entering recovery from alcohol addiction can be like trying to find your way around a big, scary forest at night, with nothing but a box of matches to light your way.

I have written this small book, *Reversing Alcoholism*, to shine a big bright light on the forest, so you see what it's really like and what actually happens to people who get into recovery.

A few years ago, I was working in an outpatient facility at a hospital in England. The service was focused on addictions. I worked with a wide range of people who had problems with a wide range of substances. Keeping up with new substances was a challenge – it is quite amazing how humanity, and in particular chemists, can keep coming up with newer ways for us to find a mental outlet, or in common parlance, get high. But there was one substance that stood out from the rest, one which affected 80% of clients in addiction and which had been around for millennia – alcohol.

My job covered carrying out clinical assessments, care planning, one-to-one counselling, and running therapeutic groups. As you can imagine, the clients could be challenging, sometimes threatening, but always rewarding to work with. However, there was one group of clients I found particularly stimulating to work with – the drinkers.

I think this was because I could relate most strongly with them. I have never smoked crack, taken ecstasy, chased the dragon, or swallowed handfuls of Diazepam. But I do know what it's like to wake up with a hangover, to have forgotten what I did the previous night, to have regretted decisions made while drunk, to have been dying for a drink without knowing why. That doesn't mean I had a problem, in fact, it probably indicates that I was a pretty normal young man at the time; since alcohol is condoned in our culture, I doubt many people grow up without having at least one experience of the negative side of drinking.

True, my negative experiences with alcohol might not have been as extreme as most of the clients I have worked with. But those experiences gave me insight into the thinking of my alcohol clients. It gave me the gifts of empathy and compassion. I could understand their confusion, pain and frustration at finding themselves in the grip of a mysterious substance that was pulling their strings like an unseen puppeteer.

Something else that fascinated me about alcohol was the diversity of problem drinkers. I find it remarkable how this particular drug, alcohol, works in so many ways with different people. My clients ranged from highly successful and rich businesspeople through to street drinkers whose lives were in total chaos.

At one end of the scale was Terry, who ran one of the largest privately-owned companies in the United Kingdom. He would arrive at work in his chauffeur-driven Bentley, passing his workers who were walking up the drive up to his grand Edwardian mansion from where he ran his business empire. When he arrived in work, his chef would make him his breakfast of eggs, bacon and mushrooms, accompanied by his first brandy of the day. Terry had just about everything a man could want, apart from happiness.

At the other end of the scale was Martin, who lived on a bench on the seafront. All his possessions were in his rucksack. I would often pass him while I was walking into work in the morning. Most days he would be clutching a large plastic bottle of cheap, rocket-fuel cider, unless he had got some money, in which case he would be drinking Jack Daniels straight from the bottle. Some days he would shout out when I passed by. Other days he would not seem to recognize me and his gaze remained fixed on the horizon. He passed his time looking out to sea, trying to keep warm, dodging the police and getting into fights with his peers.

Then there was Jenny, a well-dressed and well-spoken middle-aged mother who worked as an administrator of a college. She really wasn't the kind of person that you would suspect of having a problem, she seemed so proper. But she had half a bottle of vodka mixed in with the orange juice she kept in her bag at all times. She had also been embezzling money from the college and was full of fear that she would be found out. Her apparently comfortable, middle-class life was in danger of crashing in spectacular style.

There was Harry, who tried to keep how much he drank from his family. He was a recently-retired army officer, a big man with a big personality. He had a special long pocket inside his overcoat that was just right for him to hide a bottle of wine in. When he took the family dog out in the morning, he would insert a bottle of wine, and then drink it straight from the bottle as soon he was out of view of the house. He could drink the whole bottle in seconds. He told his family he liked exercising the dog as it kept him fit, which is why he walked it so often.

I have worked with drinkers who would only drink good wine. I have worked with drinkers who would drink mouthwash if it contained alcohol. I have worked with drinkers who were so sensitive to alcohol that a couple of glasses of wine would send them off into another world where they totally lost control. I have worked with drinkers who could consume amounts of alcohol that would kill another human being yet could carry on as if they were sober. I have worked with clients who were so extremely physically addicted to alcohol that a mere mouthful of beer would spark off the most frightening and life-threatening bender. I have worked with others were totally obsessed with alcohol but showed no signs of physical addiction. Many were pure drinkers, uninterested in other drugs. Others were cross-addicted, with alcohol being just one item on their daily drug menu.

This all goes to demonstrate that drinkers – the ones that we colloquially call alcoholics – vary enormously. Yet despite this, there is a perception that all problem drinkers are the same and there must be a similar way of treating them all.

I have to disagree. Drinkers are people, not clones. There is no universal solution that works for everyone and treating all alcoholic drinkers the same way doesn't make any sense.

Yet treatment services often try to treat them in the same way. There is a widely-held view that the way to treat dependent drinkers is to put them through detox for a week, followed by some therapy groups in aftercare for a few more weeks, and expect them to live a happy life of total abstinence thereafter. Or if drinkers go to Alcoholics Anonymous, they are expected to follow the 12-Step program, never drink again, and attend AA meetings until they die.

I would like to clarify that I am not against being abstinent from alcohol – far from it. I believe that for a minority of problem drinkers that abstinence is, in fact, the only hope for their survival. But as we will be seeing, that is not the case for everyone, and what is really going on out there is rather different from what most people believe to be true.

Also, I am not against Alcoholics Anonymous. Indeed, I have great respect for what AA has achieved over many decades, even though I believe that their program has some fundamental flaws. But

AA is nevertheless a valid form of treatment, and I am sure that it has saved the lives of thousands of people. I'm also sure it has saved innumerable marriages and careers along the way. But it is just one way of dealing with dependent drinking. Many people I meet who are AA members believe that Alcoholics Anonymous is the only way, and often argue this with a great and genuine passion. But the world of treatment is much wider than AA, or indeed any single treatment method.

Dependent drinkers are a diverse group and need to be treated as such. In fact, it sometimes seems to me that there are almost as many ways of treating dependent drinkers as there are drinkers. But this brings up the practical question of how to accommodate all this diversity, and how to coherently explain the solutions. This is what eventually brought me to writing on the subject.

In my work, I have at any one time been working with 60 or more problem drinkers on my caseload. This is far more than ideal but given the funding constraints of working in government-backed services, it had to be done. Getting to see them all regularly was a real headache, and it was a concern that the lack of time I had for each individual meant that I wasn't able to give them the level of service they needed.

One way to see all these people on a regular basis was running weekly workshops. These were well-attended, with as many as 20 drinkers in the room at any one time. But there was still too much time between them attending sessions without contact with the service – too much time for them to be able to go off-track.

What I needed, I concluded, was some sort of guide book, specific to drinkers, that they could refer to when they were alone. In this way, they would have instant access to support at any time. I thought such a book must exist. But when I searched through what was available, I was surprised to see that most books on the subject were written by people calling themselves ex-alcoholics, who wanted the reader to follow the way they had got sober.

I realized that, while these books are probably written with the best of intentions, they were fundamentally flawed and did not meet the standards needed for clients in a clinical environment.

Firstly, by promoting one particular way, this falls into the trap of a one-size-fits-all solution. Just because they had found a way that worked for them, didn't mean it would work for others, and there was no supporting research to suggest otherwise. Secondly, the writers had no clinical training, which was deeply worrying, as wrong advice given to dependent drinkers could result in a medical emergency, even death.

I found some more reliable books, written by professionals. Some were great, but none of these was quite right. Some were too academic and lacked the reader-empathy I was looking for. Some had been written in the last century and seemed too dated. Others were general to addiction and not specific to alcohol.

I concluded that the book I was looking for simply wasn't out there, and the only logical thing for me to do was to write it myself. So was born my first book, *Alcohol and You: How to Control and Stop Drinking*.

In writing that book, however, I had to be careful about what I used and left out. The reason was that that *Alcohol and You* is so information-packed that I didn't want it to become overwhelming, with too much information. Also, I realized that the topic of this book, *Reversing Alcoholism,* was too big and important to include as a chapter in *Alcohol and You*, where it might get lost among all the other chapters.

So, I present *Reversing Alcoholism* to you today as a stand-alone work. I believe that what you are about to read in this small book is important for anyone who is suffering from alcohol dependence, those already in recovery, the families and friends of problem drinkers, and workers in caring professions who want to better understand how to serve clients with such problems.

## Free PDF Download: How to Self-Diagnose Alcohol Dependency in Minutes

*Note: If you already downloaded this from Alcohol and You, you don't need to download it again.*

If you are experiencing alcohol problems, before going any further in this book, you might find it useful to answer a questionnaire that will show you where you are on the scale of alcohol dependency. To get a copy, go to subscribepage.com/drinktest.

The questionnaire is of a type widely used by clinical staff in addiction services. I use it as part of the assessment process when I see a new client. The PDF explains how it works. I hope you find it useful.

If you are reading this book because you have someone in your life that has a drink problem, or if you are a health worker, you might also like to take a look at the PDF, as I will be referring to it during the book.

# Real Recovery from Alcohol Addiction

Can alcoholism really be reversed?

Yes, it can. In fact, I believe that reversing alcoholism is a very common phenomenon. But most people are simply unaware that it happens.

When I first started working as an addiction therapist, if anyone had suggested to me that alcoholism could be reversed, I would probably have accused them of wishful thinking. I had been exposed through my work to the full horror of alcoholism. Even at the milder end of the alcoholic spectrum, I saw people who had destroyed careers and homes in their single-minded pursuit of the next drink. At the severe end of the spectrum, I worked with drinkers who had the most horrific stories to tell of the harm they had done to themselves and to others. Most shocking of all were the drinkers who carried on drinking even though physicians had told them it would kill them in months – being without a drink was more frightening than death.

Conventional wisdom was that "once an alcoholic, always an alcoholic". I was told that alcoholism was a chronic brain disease for which there was no cure. The only way of dealing with it was for the alcoholic to abstain from alcohol and spend the rest of their life in recovery.

Essentially, recovery is a strategy of containment. The ex-drinker is constantly vigilant to the risk of picking up a drink, while following a plan to keep occupied by living life in a more meaningful way. For example, "recovering alcoholics" are encouraged to refocus on work, fitness or family. For some, it means attending Alcoholics Anonymous meetings for life and following their program, the 12-Steps. For others, it could mean being in long term therapy.

For me, that isn't recovery at all. If you have an illness and you recover, the illness is gone. When most people talk about recovery in relation to alcohol, what they really mean is a life of constant maintenance, of learning how to manage the problem. But the value of recovery is not questioned as it is, without doubt, a happier outcome than being a slave to alcohol. My job was to help people get into the recovery system in the first place and then keep them there.

Some people spend their lives in recovery and are happy that way, which is great when it can be achieved. However, the weakness of recovery as a strategy lies in the word I used earlier: containment. Recovery is about containing the problem, not about solving it, as we are told there is no cure for alcoholism. And with containment, there is always the risk of the problem breaking out, or as it is generally termed, relapse.

Sadly, relapse is only too common. A frequent scenario – all too familiar to people in my type of work – is that of a drinker who spends weeks in preparation, then is detoxed, and subsequently spends weeks, sometimes months, in rehab, only to come out and start drinking almost immediately. Many will have repeated detoxes, followed by the same result.

It is widely accepted that for the alcoholic drinker, there are three outcomes.

- Drinking to destruction.
- Living in a loop of getting sober and then relapsing.
- A life of total abstinence, following a treatment plan.

But does it have to be that way? Are there other possibilities out there?

Yes, there are.

As you will see, there are huge numbers of former "alcoholics" out there who have seemingly reversed their alcoholism. They are not "in recovery". They have moved on.

In fact, as many as 75% of people who recover from alcoholism do so without ever being in treatment.

This goes a long way to explaining why the phenomenon of reversing alcoholism isn't more widely recognized. If it mostly happens outside of treatment, who knows about it? Treatment providers obviously don't know what happens with people they never meet.

If you have experienced reversing alcoholism, without being in treatment, who are you going to tell? Probably no one. More likely you will be busy getting on with your life. You may not even recognize that you were once an alcoholic, you just know you drank a lot, but now you don't.

But what about the drinkers who were in treatment? Well, if you have been in treatment and you realize you are okay and you no longer have a problem with alcohol, do you go back and report this to the staff at your drug and alcohol service, or do you just get on with your life? You probably didn't like being in treatment anyway. You will fob them off when they call you. The treatment centre can't compel you to come in, so they close your case, and you're gone.

If you have been a member of Alcoholics Anonymous and you realize you are okay now, do you go back to your AA meeting and say you are no longer an alcoholic? Pretty unlikely. You know that at AA they don't believe you can stop being an alcoholic, and you would expect a sceptical, even hostile reception from the group. So naturally, you don't go back, and no one knows. If you do meet someone from the group in the street and tell them you are okay now and don't need to go to meetings anymore, they probably won't believe you.

\*\*\*\*\*\*

So, what exactly do I mean by reversing alcoholism? Well, let's start by defining what we mean by alcoholism and an alcoholic, as we cannot define reversing if we are unclear about what it is that we are reversing.

The word alcoholic itself seems to have originated in the 19th century when it became a popular term in the temperance movement to describe a drinker. There was an alternative word, "alcoholist", which sounds rather more elegant, but that didn't stick like "alcoholic".

Personally, I don't like the terms alcoholic or alcoholism. This is partly because they are often used as insults. In treatment circles, we rarely use the word alcoholism, we more normally nowadays talk about Alcohol Use Disorder.

But the main reason why I don't like the terms alcoholism and alcoholic is that they are unspecific. How exactly do you define alcoholism? If you do a search of dictionary definitions, you will find a wide variety of definitions.

My favourite definition of alcoholism is this: *alcohol dependence*. There is a big reason why I like this definition – alcohol dependence can be *measured*. It takes away the guess-work. It takes away opinion. It is clear. What's more, it doesn't just tell you whether someone is dependent, it tells you where on the spectrum of dependence they are.

Many problem drinkers drive themselves crazy trying to decide if they are alcoholic or not. In particular, drinkers in the early days of membership of Alcoholics Anonymous can get into a stew about this, as they worry about whether to call themselves alcoholic. Although it's not compulsory to say you are an alcoholic at AA meetings (as in "Hello, my name is Joe and I'm an alcoholic.") it is the general custom. AA doesn't help in this respect, as it says the only person who can say if you're an alcoholic is you.

But it's not a simple yes or no question. It's not black and white. Alcoholism, or alcohol dependence, is a sliding scale. It would be much more helpful if, instead of worrying whether they are alcoholic, drinkers should be asking themselves how dependent they have become. Crucially, they should also be asking whether they have become physically, as well as psychologically dependent.

In my work, when I first see someone about their drinking, I carry out a clinical assessment. This is a vital first step in treatment. Without getting the full picture of what's going on with a new client, I cannot be sure I am giving them correct advice, because – as we will be discussing later in the book – alcoholism doesn't just occur in isolation. It always appears as part of a wider mix of issues. So, it's important to do my job well and serve the new client best, I find out about their medical history, prescribed medication, recreational drug use in addition to alcohol, their home life and relationships, work, hobbies, background, any history of trauma, criminal record, and so on.

But most important of all, I need to take them through a questionnaire to establish where they are on the alcohol dependence scale.

A new client might want to talk a lot, as I could be the first person they have ever honestly discussed their drinking with, and it can be a relief for some people to finally let it all out. Conversely, some people can be very guarded, especially new clients who have been coerced into seeing me in order to please their family.

Either way, it would be easy for me to be misled or come to false assumptions but using the clinical questionnaire cuts through that and gets to the truth. From a medical perspective, the score that the client comes out with from the questionnaire helps nursing staff make a judgment on whether the client needs a medically supervised detox. It's important.

The questionnaire that you were given the chance to download at the end of the last chapter is exactly the sort that is used. So, if you believe you have a drink problem and haven't downloaded it, I suggest you take a look when you've finished this chapter.

If we were able to use one of these questionnaires over time with a drinker, we could use it to establish scientifically if alcoholism reversal had taken place. For example, if I assessed a new client today, and the score showed us the client was clearly dependent, then we repeated the assessment in, say, three years from now, and the score showed us the client was no longer dependent, we would have evidence that the alcoholism had been reversed.

But waiting three years for the results from one person would not be very efficient or conclusive. To establish that alcoholism reversal exists we would need a study that:

- used a massive random sample of the population, not just people in treatment.
- was carried out by qualified professionals.
- was commissioned by a world-class organisation.

It sounds like a big ask, because if such a study already existed, surely everyone would already know about it, wouldn't they?

Does it really exist?

Yes, it does!

# The Research

In the United States, there is a government agency whose job it is to advise on alcohol misuse issues, the National Institute on Alcohol Abuse and Alcoholism (NIAAA).

Back in 1992, the NIAAA commissioned a piece of research of immense size and importance, the National Longitudinal Alcohol Epidemiologic Survey (NLAES). Staff from the United States Bureau of Census carried out face-to-face research in the field. The randomly-chosen sample was a massive 42,862 respondents.

In order to carry out the clinical assessment for Alcohol Use Disorders, the researchers used the Diagnostic and Statistical Manual of Mental Disorders, fourth edition, of the American Psychiatric Association, known for short as DSM-IV. According to the NIAAA, DSM-IV "recognizes alcohol dependence by preoccupation with drinking, impaired control over drinking, compulsive drinking, drinking despite physical or psychological problems caused or made worse by drinking, and tolerance and/or withdrawal symptoms."

The random sampling in this research gives us a great view of what is happening in the population generally. Most research on alcoholism is done with people in treatment, which gives a distorted view. I believe that drinkers in treatment tend to be at the more severe end of the alcoholic spectrum. Also, many drinkers in treatment are resistant to being helped, because they have been coerced into being there, perhaps because of family pressure, a court order, or social services intervention.

Using DSM-IV, the researchers found that around 11% of the sample were, or had been in the past, alcohol-dependent, or alcoholic in common parlance. The amazing takeaway from this research is that half of all these alcoholics were still drinking but were no longer abusing alcohol.

According to what most people believe, including people working in treatment like myself, this should not be possible: alcoholics cannot become regular drinkers. Yet, this research shows that not only can some alcoholics get over alcoholism, but also it is quite common. Alcoholism can be reversed, and often is.

Going forward ten years to 2001-2, the NIAAA followed up with the National Epidemiologic Survey on Alcohol and Related Conditions (NESARC). NESARC again sampled 43000 adults in the United

States using DSM-IV. The key highlights of this amazing body of research are:

- Most dependent drinkers fall in the mild or moderate categories. They have difficulties controlling their alcohol use, but still function in society – they have jobs and families.

- Alcohol dependence can begin any time from mid-teens until middle age, with 22 being the average age of onset.

- 72% of dependent drinkers have an episode of alcoholic drinking lasting up to four years, while the remainder can have up to five episodes of recovery and relapse back into alcoholic drinking. The NIAAA concludes that there appear to be two forms of alcohol dependence: time-limited, and recurrent or chronic.

- Twenty years after the onset of alcohol dependence, 75% of people are *in full recovery*.

- More than half of those that have achieved full recovery continue to drink, but at non-problematic levels.

This blows a big hole through what most people believe about alcoholism. Let's just look at that again: 75% are in full recovery, and over half of them are still drinking without it being problematic. Their alcoholism must have been reversed.

As Mark Willenbring, director of NIAAA's Division of Treatment and Recovery Research, said, "These and other recent findings turn on its head much of what we thought we knew about alcoholism."

The stereotypical view of the alcoholic as being a vagrant living on a park bench does have some truth in it. I have worked with people like that. But they are just a tiny minority. As Doctor Willenbring stated, "The fact is that most people who develop heavy drinking or alcohol dependence do not fit that stereotype. There are many who are not falling apart — their marriage is intact, they parent, they go to work, and in many cases, nobody even knows they are coming home and drinking a pint or more of whisky, and these people are not getting any attention at all."

But given that this vastly-important research has been around for a few years already, why is it that it isn't generally more widely known? In my experience, it isn't even that widely known among people who work in recovery.

I think the answer lies in something else that NESARC revealed: 75% of people who recover from alcohol dependence do so without ever getting any kind of help from drug and alcohol services and they never attend Alcoholics Anonymous.

The simple fact is that people working in recovery or attending AA never get to see these people. They are unaware that those people are out there. In fact, the NIAAA found that only 13% of alcoholics get specialist treatment like detox. So, the drinkers I see in my work are, as I have long suspected, at the extreme end of the alcoholic spectrum.

Also, the fact that 75% of alcoholics get well without help is an inconvenient truth for the $35-billion rehab industry. If I was running a commercial rehab, I would be keeping quiet about that.

# But Isn't It A Disease?

It has been widely accepted for decades that alcoholism is a disease, a chronic relapsing condition. What's more, it is progressive, meaning that it gets worse with time. There is no cure.

The only way to control it is to stop drinking entirely, which effectively puts you in remission. But if you subsequently drink again, you will relapse and be worse than when you stopped: because of the progressive nature of the disease, you will have got worse. Consequently, the usual advice is to become totally abstinent.

This theory, often referred to as the Disease Model, is not questioned within Alcoholics Anonymous. If you go to an AA meeting, you may well hear stories from members who have "gone back out there" (AA slang for relapse), and how it was indeed terrible, which is why they are back at an AA meeting. I am sure these people are genuine. But as we have already seen, if they are in

Alcoholics Anonymous in the first place, they are more likely to be at the extreme end of the alcohol dependency spectrum, so are more likely to have a bad relapse if they touch alcohol.

The disease model is also the cornerstone of the rehab industry, most of which, in the United States especially, uses AA's 12-Steps as part of the treatment. But again, we now see that if the people who get into rehab are likely to be at the extreme end of the alcoholic range, they are not representative of the average dependent drinker at all.

The disease model was even the received wisdom of the NIAAA until the penny dropped that their own research was telling them something very different.

According to Marc Willenbring, director of the NIAAA, "It can be a chronic, relapsing disease. But it isn't usually that."

Having worked with thousands of alcoholics, I agree with that statement. There is a minority of alcoholics for whom alcoholism is a terrifying, chronic condition. They face a stark choice between forced abstinence and early death. But for most alcoholic drinkers, it isn't like that.

In a way, it would be simpler if it was a disease. If every alcoholic suffered from the same disease, they could be treated in the same way. But they cannot. So why is alcoholism so different in different drinkers?

I believe that much of the explanation lies in that problem drinking rarely exists as a free-standing issue. It comes as part of a complex mix. Thinking about all the dependent drinkers I have worked with, I cannot remember one where alcohol has been the only issue, where everything in their life was okay except the drinking. These people were drinking because of something else.

This is where the problem drinker differs from the normal drinker. The normal, non-problematic drinker usually drinks to enhance good feelings, like having dinner with friends or to celebrate their team winning, or simply to enhance the feeling of relaxation at the end of a busy day. The problem drinker usually drinks to lessen the pain of something else that is going on, to self-medicate.

In most cases, alcohol misuse isn't the main problem; it is a *symptom* of the problem. And this is why I believe that treatment of alcoholism has such poor outcomes. If you treat the symptom, rather than the underlying issue, you might succeed in alleviating the situation for a while, but sooner or later, the underlying issue will cause the symptom of alcoholic drinking to erupt again.

The issues that lead to alcoholic drinking are many. It could be painful life events, poor thinking skills, emotional trauma, dealing with past pain, minor mental health issues such as social anxiety and overwhelm, or major ones like depression and schizophrenia. I could write a very long list, but let's look at some examples from my past caseload.

Simon was in his thirties and had recently left the army. He had a good life, a supportive wife and young children, and no money worries. He was also a fitness fanatic – except for his alcoholic binges, which were becoming so frequent there was hardly a break between them. He was panicking because he couldn't regain control. But only five minutes of talking to Simon revealed the underlying problem, as he talked about seeing his friends getting blown up in Afghanistan. He suffered from dreadful Post Traumatic Stress Disorder. He turned to the alcohol when the mental and emotional pain was too much. We could help, but the main issue was his PTSD and counselling for that was the way he would control his excess drinking in the long term.

Amanda was in her early sixties and had drunk for most of her life without alcohol being a problem. But she had been caught in a perfect storm of events beyond her control. Two close family members had died in quick succession, her husband had been diagnosed with dementia and was showing distressing signs of deterioration, and she had to wind up her husband's business. Her drinking had escalated to help her cope with feelings of profound emotional pain and overwhelm. She came into treatment when she realized that she had lost control of her drinking. We could help in as much as teaching her some skills to control her drinking, and getting her a prescription for Nalmefene to lessen the desire to drink. But clearly, this was just treating the symptom. The cure came in her getting support around her life issues. Her life became less overwhelming as her grief lessened, she got support with her husband, and her husband's company was sold. Eventually, she stopped drinking altogether, not because she felt she had to, but simply because she lost interest in it. She had her life back.

Jeannine was in her forties and had been drinking to unconsciousness every day. At one time, she had been manager of a health foods store, but her self-neglect had become so acute that she had been admitted to hospital with malnutrition. She had lost almost all interest in eating. Her diet consisted mainly of cider and vodka. Her drinking had become heavy after her husband left her for another woman 10 years earlier. She had had time to get over losing him, but she could not let go of the sense of injustice, frequently saying how much she had done for him and how unfair it was. Jeannine's mind was constantly on the lookout for evidence of how unfair life was to her and for further outrages to fuel her sense of injustice, which in turn stoked her desire to drink to oblivion. Jeannine's mind was in a loop. The more she looked for outrages against her, the more she found them, which in turn encouraged her to look for yet more. Seeing that her drinking was a symptom of her self-defeating thinking, we set her on a course of intensive CBT. Jeannine started to identify that she could not prevent life from being unfair, but she had, if she desired, total control over her responses to life's injustices. She also began to grasp that by constantly looking for what was wrong, she was not noticing what was right, such as the love of her grown-up son. It took time, but Jeannine began taking responsibility for herself, rather than looking to blame everyone else for her troubles. Her self-esteem grew, she started to take care of herself and she revived her interest in a healthy lifestyle. New people came into her life, attracted by her sunnier disposition, and opportunities started to open up for her. One day she announced she had stopped drinking, saying she didn't need it anymore. She didn't stay abstinent long term but just drank on a very occasional basis. The compulsive urge to drink to oblivion had departed with her sense of outrage.

These examples are people who had all been drinking to levels diagnosable as dependent, but who had in different ways shown that they could move on, quite naturally, without having to be in life-long treatment. Dealing with their underlying problems had been how they had turned things around, rather than completely focusing on their drinking, which was merely the symptom.

These types of dependent drinkers are typical of the bulk of people who have alcohol problems. However, in order to give a complete picture, I should also talk about two client groups that are more complex and less likely to achieve alcoholism reversal.

The first group of drinkers are those people who are physically dependent as well as psychologically dependent on alcohol. These are a minority, and it is interesting to contrast how different alcohol is to another very common drug in this respect, namely nicotine. Most people who smoke do so because they have a severe physical dependence, but not usually a strong psychological one. I have experienced first-hand just how severe nicotine addiction is, as I was a smoker for many years. The withdrawal I experienced when I stopped was horrific, and much of my motivation for never smoking since is that I never want to go through that again. Most smokers want to quit.

By contrast, the majority of alcoholic drinkers are not strongly physically dependent – we know this because they don't exhibit strong symptoms of withdrawal if they stop and don't require detox. They have what Alcoholics Anonymous calls the mental obsession, and I would agree with AA on that description. Most of the training I have done for working with drinkers has centred on physiological tools, whereas training I have done for smoking cessation has hardly mentioned this, focusing instead on dealing with cravings and nicotine replacement therapies. Also, in contrast to smokers who mostly want to quit, these drinkers mostly don't want to stop.

Drinkers who have both a strong physical dependence and the mental obsession have a much more difficult time than the majority and may find that alcoholic reversal unachievable. For those who are physically dependent, stopping drinking without treatment is very dangerous. I do not think it is either sensible or ethical for me to suggest that every alcoholic can move on from alcohol dependence. For the minority, an abstinence-based strategy of containment is likely to be the safest option.

The classic signs of physical dependence are daily drinking, starting drinking early in the day, shaking in the morning before having the first drink, and heavy sweating, often waking up drenched in sweat. Physically dependent drinkers run the risk of seizure, which can be life-threatening if they don't drink regularly, because their bodies have become so dependent on having a level of alcohol in the system, that the body starts to malfunction if that level isn't maintained. This is why some drinkers need to be detoxed under medical supervision. If you think this describes you, please go and see a physician or a counsellor at your local drug and alcohol service without delay.

The second group of drinkers who have a less optimistic prognosis are dual diagnosis clients. These are people with a mental health diagnosis that requires psychiatric support, in addition to alcohol dependence. In particular, paranoid schizophrenia and the more severe forms of depression can be challenging to work with, and these will usually come with other issues, such as severe anxiety, psychosis, and often poly-drug addiction. Progress can be made with this client group, but it requires a coordinated effort from medical, psychiatric and addiction services, and as such is beyond the scope of this book.

# Drinking and Addiction

Using alcohol as a way of alleviating emotion suffering is a huge cause of problem drinking. But drinking as a hard-wired habit – an addiction – is another and quite separate cause.

To understand this, let's look first at what an addict and an addiction actually are. To most people, the word addict conjures up images of illicit drug users, but this is misleading. A useful definition of an addict would be someone who pursues one particular source of pleasure to the detriment of vital aspects of their life. The addiction is whatever that source of pleasure is.

Human beings are generally prone to addiction. In fact, it is quite amazing just how many things we humans can get addicted to. For example, we can get addicted to gambling, console games, sex, smartphones, shopping, violence, social media, working, exercising, shoplifting, starting fires, dieting, and watching television – all manner of things that don't include putting a drug into your body.

Looking at gambling as an example, this isn't a problem for most people. Many of us never gamble at all. For other people, it might be a small flutter on the state lottery or putting a small wager on a horse in a big race once a year. But if someone is gambling to such an extent that it takes up most of their thinking, their relationships are suffering, they are losing so much money that they are running up big credit card debts and missing mortgage payments, then they are meeting my definition of an addict, because they are gambling to the detriment of vital aspects of their life.

If someone with a gambling addiction is challenged about what they are doing, rather than stopping gambling, it's likely that they will just start hiding their habit and find ways of gambling in secret. Interestingly, this is exactly the sort of behaviour that dependent drinkers usually do, if they are challenged about their drinking. They usually start hiding their drinking rather than facing up to it.

But how about watching television? That sounds harmless enough, and for most people it is. But if someone is watching television for most of their waking hours, they are neglecting their health through lack of exercise and maybe compounding the problem by becoming obese through eating comfort food while they watch. If their relationships are also suffering because they are not giving them enough attention, or if their work or studies are suffering because they don't give them enough time, then that person has met my definition of an addict. They are watching television to the detriment of vital aspects of their life.

If you imagine a situation where a television addict had their television taken away for a night, that person would probably become agitated, short-tempered and stressed. They might even show physical symptoms like sweating and churning in the stomach. They would find it difficult to think about the one thing they don't have – the television. This is exactly the sort of effect that being without a drink for a night would have on an alcoholic, except they would be thinking about the drink they are missing, rather than Netflix or their favourite game show.

We talk about addiction to alcohol, but I think that the real addiction goes wider than just alcohol. It is an obsession with the whole business of drinking, of which the alcohol itself is just one component. There is the whole paraphernalia of drinking, the attractive bottles and labels, the different types of glasses, books on drinking, the endless varieties of vineyards or brands, advertising, the locations, the favourite bars, the glistening rows of bottles behind the bar, the favourite bar stool, the regular drinking buddies you meet up with. Above all, for most dependent drinkers, there is the deeply ingrained routine: starting drinking at the same time, going to the same regular haunts, meeting the same people.

It all adds up to a really compelling mix of stimulation and behaviours that create an addiction – and that's before we have even taken into account actually drinking any alcohol. That's also before we have factored in any emotional pain that might be driving the drinking. And that's even before we have considered whether there is any physical dependency involved.

This is why dependent drinking is such an intractable problem and why people relapse. It is more than just removing the alcohol. Even if a drinker has been detoxed and is clean of any alcohol in the body, this compelling mix that makes up the addiction is still there, and why simply dealing with the alcohol in isolation is unlikely to be successful. Alcoholism is about more than alcohol. It's about the whole package. It's when the package has been dealt with that we can see real recovery from alcohol addiction.

# Important New Book from Lewis David: "The 10-Day Alcohol Detox Plan"

I wrote "Alcohol and You" so that drinkers could make an informed choice on how to deal with their alcohol issues.

Since then, I have been asked many times to write my default strategy – something that works for everyone.

"The 10-Day Alcohol Detox Plan" is that book.

This book is for anyone, whether you want to take a break from drinking or stop forever.

It's also for drinkers who want to cut down, because research shows that you stand a much better chance of reducing if you have a complete break from drinking for a short time first.

When you stop drinking, it takes up to 10 days for every trace of alcohol to leave your system. This is a tricky time. As the alcohol level in your body drops, you experience cravings and your thinking becomes more emotional. Consequently, most drinkers who fail to quit do so in those first 10 days.

"The 10-Day Alcohol Detox Plan" is designed to walk you through the critical early days, making the process easy and even enjoyable. All you have to do is read the book during the 10 days.

It will reinforce what you have learned in "Alcohol and You" and also introduce you to new ideas I have worked on since writing that book.

To learn more and read a free sample, go to my website WinsPress.com, or enter this product code into the search bar of any Amazon site (Amazon.com, Amazon.co.uk etc): B07YRSFW15

**THE 10-DAY ALCOHOL DETOX PLAN**

Lewis David

# **Finally…**

That brings us to the end of the bonus chapters and the end of this book.

If you have found "Alcohol and You" helpful, I would be massively grateful if you could review this book on Amazon.

Your review could make a difference and help put this book into the hands of someone who needs it.

Thank you for reading "Alcohol and You."

Printed in Great Britain
by Amazon